DISCOVERING A WELSH LANDSCAPE

Landscapes of Britain

Britain has an extraordinarily rich mix of historic landscapes. This major series explores this diversity, through accessible and attractive books that draw on the latest archaeological and historical research. Places in Britain have a great depth of historical connections. These books show how much there is to be discovered.

Also in this series

John Barnatt and Ken Smith, *The Peak District: Landscapes Through Time*
N. J. Higham, *A Frontier Landscape: The North West in the Middle Ages*
Robert Van de Noort, *The Humber Wetlands: The Archaeology of a Dynamic Landscape*

Discovering a Welsh Landscape

Archaeology in the Clwydian Range

Ian Brown
with photographs by Mick Sharp and Jean Williamson

WIND*gather*
PRESS

Discovering a Welsh Landscape: Archaeology in the Clwydian Range

© Denbighshire County Council, 2004

Published by: Windgather Press Ltd, 29 Bishop Road, Bollington,
Macclesfield, Cheshire SK10 5NX, UK

Distributed by: Central Books Ltd, 99 Wallis Road, London E9 5LN

British Library Cataloguing-in-Publication Data
A catalogue record for this book is available from the British Library

ISBN 0-9545575-7-3

Designed, typeset and originated by Carnegie Publishing Ltd,
Chatsworth Road, Lancaster
Printed and bound by Cambridge University Press

Contents

List of Figures

All photographs are copyright Mick Sharp and Jean Williamson unless otherwise indicated.

Discovering a Welsh Landscape: Archaeology in the Clwydian Range

Acknowledgements

Many people have influenced the content of this book from its early inception and all my colleagues of the Countryside, Archaeology and Museum Services of the former Clwyd County Council and those of the Clwyd/Powys Archaeological Trust, with whom we worked, deserve a special mention from the outset. Likewise do members of the Department of Archaeology and Anthropology of the University of Wales, Lampeter, especially Professor David Austin, and those of the Institute of Archaeology at the University of Oxford. In particular I am indebted to Professor Barry Cunliffe, my supervisor at Oxford, without whom my passion for archaeology would not have been ignited.

Special thanks must be given to members and officers of the Clwydian Range Area of Outstanding Natural Beauty Joint Advisory Committee, who backed the book from the beginning, and the Welsh Assembly Government and Countryside Council for Wales, from whom generous funds were forthcoming from the Environment Development Fund for its writing and production. Howard Sutcliffe, Huw Rees and David Shiel of the Denbighshire Countryside Service, Fiona Gale, County Archaeologist of Denbighshire and Trefor Thompson of Denbighshire County Council all deserve special mention, as does my former colleague John Ablitt.

I would also like to thank the following for their valuable assistance in the various stages of the project: John Blore for images of his impressive finds at Lynx Cave and discussions on his work; the Rectors of the churches of St Mary, Cilcain, St Mary, Gwaenysgor, St Garmon, Llanarmon yn Iâl, Corpus Christi, Tremeirchion and St Mael and St Sulien at Cwm; Father McGuiness for information about St Beuno's; Mick and Jan Fenwick of the Ffynnon Beuno Country House, Tremeirchion, which is well worth a visit, for access to the cave sites; Nigel Steele-Mortimer of the Golden Grove estate, Captain Archdale of Penbedw and all the other landowners in the Clwydian Range who have been most helpful during all aspects of the work.

Also grateful thanks to Peter Boyd of the Shrewsbury Museums Service, Eva Bredsdorff of the Powysland Museum, Welshpool, Adam Gwilt of the National Museums and Galleries of Wales, John Prag of the Manchester Museum, Dan Robinson of the Grosvenor Museum, Chester and the County Archivist of Flintshire County Council for assistance in providing excellent photographs from the collections of their respective institutions, all of which have been credited in the text.

Finally I would like to thank Mick Sharp and Jean Williamson for the fine photographs used throughout, Paddie Morrison for the excellent illustrations, John Shillam for valuable assistance with fieldwork and my mother for encouraging me to write the book in the first place.

Discovering a Welsh Landscape: Archaeology in the Clwydian Range

Dedicated to my father,
William Brown,
who loved north Wales

Preface

As we walked along the hills towards it [Moel Famau] the valley
looked more charming and touching than ever ... The day was
then treatening and clouded, the sea and distant hills brimmed
with purple, clouds trailing low, the landscape clear but sober ...
(Gerard Manley Hopkins 1876)

This book is intended to introduce those interested in their cultural and
environmental heritage to one corner of north-east Wales, the Clwydian
Range of hills, designated an Area of Outstanding Natural Beauty in 1985. Its
archaeology was outlined, in part, in the 'Archaeology of Clwyd' published by
Clwyd County Council in 1991. It is not intended to repeat this compre-
hensive review. Instead, using selective narrative and photographs,
complimented where necessary by reference to sites and events outside the
area, this book aims to show how this strategically situated, richly varied and
outstanding landscape has figured prominently in the past history of the
British Isles.

It is hoped that, encouraged by this introduction, the reader will feel
confident enough to delve more deeply into heritage studies and to get
involved *on the ground*; and perhaps to investigate the archaeology and landscape of the Clwydian Range itself. Archaeology and history are not elite
subjects, as the continued popularity of television programmes shows. They
are there to be shared by everyone.

CHAPTER I

A Border Country

About three miles to the north is a range of lofty mountains, dividing the shire of Denbigh from that of Flint, amongst which, almost parallel with the town, and lifting its head high above the rest, is the mighty Moel Vamagh, the mother heap, which I had seen from Chester. (George Borrow (1862), 83)

The nearness of the Clwydian Range to the Welsh border with England is apparent in this line from George Borrow, who between August and November 1854 travelled from north to south Wales. In the tradition of Victorian landscape and social enquirers, his journey culminated in the publication of a book, *Wild Wales*, in 1862. Although he did not venture into the area we know today as the Clwydian Range (colloquially called the 'Clwyds' or 'Clwydians'), he was clearly fascinated by the 'mighty Moel Vamagh', or Moel Famau as it is now called, the highest point in this 35-kilometre line of undulating hills, extending from the Nant y Garth Pass, north of Llangollen in the south, to Prestatyn and the Irish Sea in the north (Figures 1 and 2).

It is this proximity to England which has moulded the social and cultural landscape of the area throughout historical times and which has seen waves of change take place from east to west across the border between the two countries. North-east Wales, of which the Clwyds form a significant part, is 'border country' and forms the northern-most segment of the Welsh Marches, which extend from the estuary of the River Dee in the north to the Severn Estuary in the south. The Anglo-Saxon word for 'boundary' is *mearc* and it is from this that 'march' is probably derived.

The landscape with which we are concerned extends across the rising shelving plateau of Flintshire, west of the Dee, to the crest of the Clwydian Range before plunging down to the Vale of Clwyd. It has been the scene of many foreign incursions since the time of Christ, and most of them have had a lasting impact on the Celtic culture which had developed over the preceding millennia. These incursions have been in turn Roman, Anglo-Saxon, Scandinavian and Anglo-Norman, and have all imposed their individual identities on a landscape that is still continually changing today.

Sandwiched between the powerful kingdom of Gwynedd to the west and Anglo-Saxon Mercia and later the Palatinate of Chester to the east, by the end

FIGURE 1.
The undulating hills of the Clwydian Range from the Vale of Clwyd.

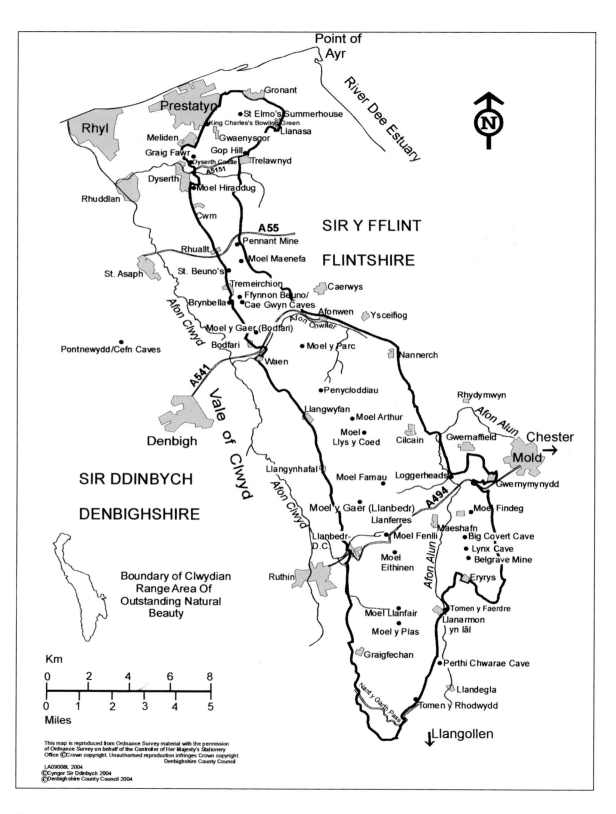

Point of
Ayr

River Dee Estuary

Gronant

Prestatyn

Rhyl

St Elmo's Summerhouse
King Charles's Bowling Green
Meliden
Llanasa
Gwaenysgor
Graig Fawr
Gop Hill
Dyserth Castle
Trelawnyd
A5151
Dyserth
Moel Hiraddug

Rhuddlan

Cwm

A55   SIR Y FFLINT

Rhuallt
Pennant Mine

Moel Maenefa   FLINTSHIRE

St. Asaph
St. Beuno's

Tremeirchion   Caerwys

Ffynnon Beuno/
Brynbella   Cae Gwyn Caves

Afon Chwiler   Afonwen   Ysceifiog

Moel y Gaer (Bodfari)

Pontnewydd/Cefn Caves
Bodfari   Moel y Parc   Nannerch

Waen

Rhydymwyn

Penycloddiau

Afon Alun   Chester

Llangwyfan   Moel Arthur

Moel   Cilcain   Gwernaffield   Mold
Llys y Coed

Denbigh

Gwernymynydd

SIR DDINBYCH   Llangynhafal   Moel Famau   Loggerheads
A494

DENBIGHSHIRE   Moel y Gaer (Llanbedr)   Moel Findeg

Llanferres   Maeshafn

Llanbedr-   Moel Fenlli   Big Covert Cave
D.C   Lynx Cave
Moel   Belgrave Mine
Eithinen
Eryrys

Ruthin
Tomen y Faerdre
Moel Llanfair   Llanarmon
yn Iâl
Moel y Plas
Perthi Chwarae Cave
Graigfechan
Llandegla

Nant y Garth Pass
Tomen y Rhodwydd

Llangollen

Boundary of Clwydian
Range Area Of
Outstanding Natural
Beauty

Km
0   2   4   6   8
0   1   2   3   4   5
Miles

This map is reproduced from Ordnance Survey material with the permission
of Ordnance Survey on behalf of the Controller of Her Majesty's Stationery
Office ©Crown copyright. Unauthorised reproduction infringes Crown copyright.
Denbighshire County Council

LA09008L 2004
©Cyngor Sir Ddinbych 2004
©Denbighshire County Council 2004

4

of the twelfth century the title *y Berfeddwlad* (the 'Middle Country') had been bestowed on the area between the Afon Conwy and the River Dee. The land was for centuries a battleground between the English and Welsh, and it was not until the statutes of 1536 and 1542 that the area had any semblance of cultural and administrative stability.

The border character had become apparent much earlier in prehistory, and the imposing Iron Age hillforts astride the high Clwydians testify to a continuum of human activity that has imposed its presence on the landscape from the very earliest times. North-east Wales shows substantial evidence of a thriving Bronze Age and Neolithic culture and is one of the most important places in western Europe for evidence of human activity in the Palaeolithic.

This continual ebb and flow of peoples from east to west rather than from north to south is still much in evidence today. It is still easier to travel eastwards to Chester than southwards to Cardiff. These lines of flow have influenced cultural development and large numbers of people live in the Clwydian Range and commute to the conurbations of Merseyside, west Cheshire and Manchester, and the new bridge over the Dee at Queensferry has stimulated this historical trend. Whilst the area is undoubtedly rural and agricultural in character, only a small number of workers are employed in farming nowadays. The traditional isolation of these northern marchlands continues to be broken down as ease of access increases.

The moorland crest of the Clwydians remains, however, as 'wild' as any comparable landscape can be nowadays and the development of both Welsh and English settlements, a reflection of the troubled history of the border, is manifested in both 'townships' with a traditional Welsh pattern and with a pattern altered by continual immigration from England.

The landscape of narrow embanked lanes, interspaced with hamlet and small village-type settlement, has also been substantially altered since the First World War by extensive quarry workings in the areas where limestone outcrops (Figure 3). Overgrown and hidden lead-workings speak of substantial industrial activity in the past. Since Roman times, but especially in the eighteenth and nineteenth centuries, industry has had a dominating and economically productive influence on the landscape. Through-routes for major transportation links from England to north-west Wales and across the Irish Sea have also left their mark.

In the midst of all of this turmoil the outstanding quality of the landscape shines through. It is an ancient landscape, but above all it is a landscape of change.

The natural landscape

FIGURE 2. Location map of the Clwydian Range and principal sites.

Mountains and high moorland dominate the landscape of Wales; more than half of the land area being over 200 metres O.D. and much over 600 metres. North-east Wales, however, varies from less than 50 metres O.D. in the coastal plain in the north, to between 100 and 200 metres in the gently-sloping

landscape of east Flintshire bordering the Dee Estuary and between 200 and 500 metres in the high hills of the Clwydian Range itself. Here the peaks increase in height from Moel Hiraddug above the coastal plain in the north at 264 metres O.D. to Moel Famau at 555 metres O.D. (Figure 4).

Rock structure broadly influences landform locally, but Wales mainly owes its upland character to uplift during the Tertiary and the hardness of its strata. A series of dissected plateau surfaces forms the outstanding features of the country, the Flintshire Plateau, flanking the east of the high Clwydian summits, being one example. The Clwyds are too dissected to be called 'plateaux' as such and are termed by Brown (1960) 'hills', being restricted in area but geologically diverse.

The central spine of the Clwydian Range is composed of highly folded grits, shales, flags and mudstones, interbedded with bands of sandstone of the Valentinian-Wenlock-Ludlow series of the Middle Silurian. The formations vary in thickness, sometimes extending to many hundreds of metres, and their distribution and mode of occurrence create great variety in the landscape.

The hills of the Clwyds are a north-south trending anticline and syncline,

FIGURE 3.
Burley Hill quarry set amongst important early hominid sites.

6

the western (anticline) limb of this fold truncated by the Vale of Clwyd fault, induced during Hercynian (post-Carboniferous) times. It is the largely Hercynian horst and graben topography (ie. the network of normal faults dividing the rocks into blocks of different sizes) which, after being moulded by ice action, give the Range its distinctive appearance today. The major features of the high Clwydian scarp-line and neighbouring areas are, therefore, a reflection of this underlying geology and in particular of the Hercynian faulting which created the Vale of Clwyd to the west and uplifted the hills themselves.

There are three main advances of glaciation recognised in Britain – the Anglian, Wolstonian and Devensian. Before the Anglian and between succeeding glaciations, there were interglacial periods – the Cromerian, Hoxnian and Ipswichian. The warmer period following the Devensian, the Flandrian or Holocene, is the period we now live in, itself in all probability just another interglacial period. Things are complicated by the fact that within each glacial and each interglacial were shorter warmer and colder phases respectively. In fact, going back 700,000 years, some eight glacial periods have been recognised (Darvill 1987, 28).

FIGURE 4.
Moel Famau. The highest point in the Clwydian Range at 555 metres O.D.

Many features of the landscape betray a more recent glacial and periglacial landforming phase. Of the major ice ages that affected the Clwydian Range during the Quaternary, only the most recent (Devensian) glaciation, of about 18,000 years ago, is apparent in the geomorphology, although distinct phases of glacial action and warmer inter-stadial periods are known within this glaciation and little is known about earlier glaciations. The last ice left north Wales around 14,000 years ago (Jenkins 1991, 19). North-east Wales is important as an area of influence and confrontation of both 'Welsh' and 'Irish Sea' Ice and, as a result, many landforms are representative of slow-moving, stagnant and decaying ice-sheets.

Ice has itself sculpted the Range, but to the west the Vale of Clwyd is composed of sandstones and marls laid down during the dry conditions of the Permian. These rocks are relatively soft and produce exceptionally fertile soils. The Clwydian Range probably did not generate its own glaciers and any immature cirques present in the Range, and most notably on the eastern flank of Moel Famau, are probably nivation hollows caused by freeze-thaw action and solifluction on the edge of persistent snow patches (Brown, Ratcliffe and Hawkes 1979, 12).

The area, then, was instead engulfed by ice-sheets emanating from Snowdonia in the west and the Arenigs in the south during the main phase of the last glaciation. The northern ice sheets came up the Vale of Clwyd to within 5 kilometres of Denbigh and created a terminal moraine across the vale at Trefnant. Here a glacial lake, known as 'Lake Clwyd', was formed by meltwaters and stretched for some 10 kilometres to the south of Llanfair DC. Deltas built-up where rivers and streams entered the lake from the Denbigh Moors; for example at Aberchwiler by the Afon Chwiler. When Lake Clwyd finally filled with sediment is unclear, but it is possible that small lakes and vestiges of alder carr existed in the fifth millennium BC when the first evidence of human activity on open sites in the vale appeared (CPAT 2003).

Although the general movement of the ice was north-westwards, much of the Welsh Ice was directed northwards along the Vale of Conwy and eastwards along the Dee valley. Therefore the ice that spilled across the Denbigh Moors filling the Vale of Clwyd, was relatively slow moving, and was further prevented from any appreciable northward movement by the southern boundary of the Irish Sea Ice. At a later stage of the Devensian glaciation, when Welsh Ice had retreated from the Denbigh Moors and Vale of Clwyd, the Irish Sea Ice pushed far inland leaving glacial erratics of Lake District origin near to Denbigh itself. Although ice movement in the main part of the Vale of Clwyd was minimal, some transverse movement of ice did occur eastwards across the Clwydian Range, resulting in blocks from the Arenigs near Bala found in the Moel Famau Country Park. A series of *roche moutonnée* landforms are incorporated in the southern perimeter of Penycloddiau hillfort. They consist of rock outcrops smoothed by the ice on the upper surface and showing a jagged ice-plucked surface where the ice had retreated, so indicating a localised movement of the Welsh Ice in the area (Brown, Ratcliffe and Hawkes 1979, 15).

FIGURE 5.
Landscape character map of the Clwydian Range (after Denbighshire County Council 2000).

8

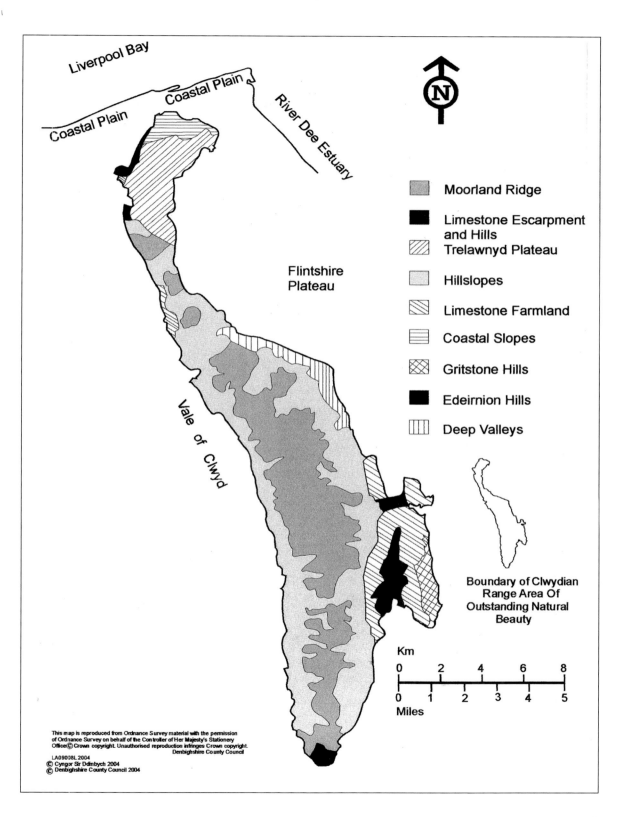

Liverpool Bay

Coastal Plain

Coastal Plain

River Dee Estuary

N

Flintshire
Plateau

Vale of Clwyd

Moorland Ridge

Limestone Escarpment
and Hills

Trelawnyd Plateau

Hillslopes

Limestone Farmland

Coastal Slopes

Gritstone Hills

Edeirnion Hills

Deep Valleys

Boundary of Clwydian
Range Area Of
Outstanding Natural
Beauty

Km

0   2   4   6   8

0 1   2   3   4   5

Miles

This map is reproduced from Ordnance Survey material with the permission
of Ordnance Survey on behalf of the Controller of Her Majesty's Stationery
Office© Crown copyright. Unauthorised reproduction infringes Crown copyright.
Denbighshire County Council

LA09008L 2004
© Cyngor Sir Ddinbych 2004
© Denbighshire County Council 2004

9

The depth and symmetry of the Vale of Clwyd itself is the result of Hercynian rift valley faulting rather than glacial action, but to the east the lateral movement of ice across the Clwydian Range is responsible for the U-shaped deepening of valleys and the smooth U-shaped cols of Bwlch Pen Barras and Bwlch-y-Frainc, which have proved, as we shall see, so significant in archaeological terms.

Few parts of the Range are free from glacial drift, apart from the peaks of the hills, although it tends to be obscured by post-glacial peat or head deposits. The Welsh Ice drift, which is a common feature, is a rubbly till, incorporating yellowish-brown shaly Silurian material and ice-scratched Ordovician boulders, whilst the Triassic Bunter Sandstone of the Vale of Clwyd has contributed reddish sands to the deposits of the high Range.

The incised valley of the Chwiler-Alun gap, where sub-glacial drainage escaped initially from the Vale of Clwyd, cuts through the Clwydian Range itself and the lower Flintshire Plateau and the Carboniferous Limestone underlies most of the area to the north, south and east of the Silurian scarp. These Carboniferous beds dip to the east, the limestone with its rich veins of lead and zinc with varying degrees of silver forming the westerly, higher parts of

FIGURE 6.
The Clwydian Range from Moel Arthur, one of the great Clwydian hillforts straddling the 'Moorland Ridge'.

FIGURE 7.
Bryn Alun. A fine and characteristic 'Limestone Escarpment and Hills' landscape of great archaeological significance from the Palaeolithic to the modern era.

the plateau, whilst the Coal Measures, with rich coal and ironstone deposits, form both the eastern flanks and the coastal platforms.

The massive grey bioclastic Carboniferous Limestone of the Lower Carboniferous is a prominent feature around the former Flint and Denbigh coalfield and, as we shall see, has had a profound influence on the archaeology of the area. These D-facies limestones in north Wales contain considerable quantities of chert, used extensively in the area for tool manufacture in prehistory. Some may have been deposited on the Dinantian sea floor as coloidal silica, but it is also thought to have been secondary in origin, as oolitic and other textures and fossils have been found pseudo-morphed in silica (Wells and Kirkaldy 1966, 218).

The overlying drift geology is a result of climatic fluctuations and associated glacial actions over the last 1.6 million years. This has resulted in the deposition of sands and gravels, particularly along the eastern edge and the river valleys, leading to their extraction for use in the building industries. In general, the limestone plateau is gentle and undulating in contrast to the steeper slopes of the Silurian ridge. The Coal Measures carried woodland even in the eleventh century, but the areas of limestone and Silurian tracts are open by nature, interspaced with more sheltered and richer stream valleys.

The character of the landscape

The Clwydian Range shows a kaleidoscope of landscape types. In the Clwyd Landscape Assessment of 1995 (Denbighshire County Council 2000), nine 'Character Areas' were identified (Figure 5), each showing similar characteristics of geology, topography, ecology, field and settlement pattern, and these are outlined below.

Moorland Ridge
The moorland ridge is the dominant and outstanding landscape type within the Clwydian Range and forms mostly heather-clad hills stretching along the upland crest. Moel Famau and outstanding examples of Iron Age hillforts dominate the landscape (Figure 6). Open heather moorland is very important in the Clwyds, especially in the southern half of the area, where extensive areas of common and traditional moorland estate exist. The vegetation also comprises bilberry, gorse and bracken with a few areas of semi-natural acid grassland, the whole comprising a traditional mosaic or 'ffrith', so important to landscape and wildlife alike.

Large areas of the hills have been reclaimed for agriculture, creating conspicuous grassland slopes which interrupt the heather moorland. Likewise, large coniferous forests have been established, as at Llangwyfan below Moel Arthur and below Moel Famau, altering the landscape locally. To the north the character of the hills is less open and windswept, becoming more pastoral as a result of agriculture and forestry plantings. Fragments of moorland and bracken survive on the highest points, together with significant areas of broadleaved woodland which clothe certain slopes, as near Bodfari in the Afon Chwiler valley.

Limestone Escarpment and Hills

The limestone areas of Prestatyn Hillside, Graig Fawr and Dyserth Mountain in the north and Loggerheads, Maeshafn and Llanarmon yn Iâl in the south are especially important for archaeology and form rugged hills with scarp faces, rock outcrops and limestone pavements (Figure 7).

The open limestone grasslands are variably rich in native wild flowers, depending on the degree of agricultural improvement. The lower steep slopes below the scarp face were formerly covered with native broad-leaved woodland, some of which has now been planted with conifer plantation, as at Maeshafn. On the western side of the main ridge prominent limestone outcrops jut out at Tremeirchion and Graigfechan and are mostly grazed, but at Prestatyn Hillside lack of open grazing and natural colonisation of scrub poses a management problem, altering the landscape's open character.

The limestone gorges of the River Alun are a spectacular addition to what is a typical karst landscape, the river disappearing underground in dry weather. Extensive valley woodlands are also a distinctive feature of the river and steep woodland slopes predominate as at Loggerheads, with grassy slopes occasionally containing pockets of unimproved pasture. Here lime-loving plants, such as cowslips and orchids, are found.

Trelawnyd Plateau

Away from the main limestone to the north, the Trelawnyd Plateau stretches to the east and south (Figure 8). This extensive plateau is underlain by Carboniferous Limestone which, although restricted in outcrop, forms the main constituent building material for many of the vernacular houses and walls. Gop Hill dominates the surrounding plateau and a mixture of ancient and more recent field patterns is a distinguishing characteristic. Relatively small blocks of conifer planting have a marked effect on local character. Past mining and its influences are evident, with a high concentration of prehistoric and industrial archaeological remains. The Trelawnyd Plateau was an important area in the prehistoric period and Bronze Age burial mounds and small enclosures are well represented.

Hillslopes

On the western side of the Clwydian Range, steep hillslopes of enclosed farm-land meet open stretches of moorland and bracken on both sides of the moorland ridge. Fields are mostly small and irregular in form and often edged with overgrown hedgerows, whilst small ancient woodlands occur in narrow valleys and hillsides. On the eastern side of the Range above the Alun Valley, a similar landscape type predominates, although it has been more influenced by agricultural improvement. As a result fields are larger and local woodland

FIGURE 8 (*opposite*). The 'Trelawnyd Plateau' near Gop Hill; an area of much Neolithic activity.

FIGURE 9. Limekilns characterise the 'Limestone Farmland' areas, as this example near Tremeirchion shows.

FIGURE 10. Moel Findeg in the 'Gritstone Hills'. Formerly a source of mineral wealth, now a nature conservation and recreation site.

FIGURE 11.
The Nant y Garth Pass
characterises the 'Deep
Valleys' landscape area
in the far south of the
Clwydian Range.

is sparse, with hedgerow trees more typically in decline, the majority being mature or over mature.

Limestone Farmland

The enclosed limestone farmlands are characterised by mostly small-scale, often geometric, field patterns, typical of more recent enclosure, and are mostly bounded by stone walls. Occasional limestone outcrops are evident in the landscape. The character of all of the limestone areas of the Clwydian Range has been much influenced by past mining and industrial activity, which has left remains of small disused quarries, mine shafts, mine spoil and old lime kilns (Figure 9). Other characteristic features include many stone-built buildings, narrow lanes and herb-rich banks and verges. More recent intrusions in the landscape are the large modern quarries at Dyserth and Maeshafn.

Coastal Slopes

To the south-east of Prestatyn the land drops from the northern edge of the Clwydian Range in distinct pastoral slopes to the coastal and estuary strip below. Where slopes are steeper and in narrow valleys, semi-natural broadleaved woodlands give a mosaic effect to the landscape. Medium-size irregular fields are defined by well-maintained hedgerows and hedgerow trees are common. Settlement is generally confined to scattered farms and small cottages.

Gritstone Hills

To the east of Maeshafn and Eryrys to the south, an intricate and traditional landscape of distinct and rolling hills with deep and often wooded valleys, is characterised by a mosaic of small hedged-fields and woods and pockets of semi-natural vegetation (Figure 10). Narrow winding lanes link small villages, farms and cottages. Millstone Grit is the predominant building stone for many of the older buildings. The diverse semi-natural vegetation includes woods, scrub, bracken and wetlands.

Edeirnion Hills

To the south of the Nant y Garth Pass, a strongly undulating rural landscape of rounded and interlocking hills is found, with large irregular fields defined by overgrown hedgerows and sparse tree cover. This is a landscape of rolling hills and valley slopes, with remote farms linked by narrow and winding lanes. Woodland is largely absent and there are few hedgerow trees. Fields are generally large and irregular and farmland is generally improved, with packets of rough grassland and wetland.

Deep Valleys

The deep narrow valley of the fast-flowing Afon Chwiler in the middle of the Range and the Nant y Garth Pass to the far south, both show well-wooded slopes interspersed with bracken, scrub and unintensive farmland contrasting strongly with the adjacent moorland landscape (Figure 11). The valley sides often have a broadleaved and coniferous woodland interspaced with bracken, rough pasture and gorse, with less intensively farmed fields. These are major communications routes, with small villages and wayside cottages. The Chwiler valley was formerly the line of the Mold and Denbigh Junction Railway, and active quarrying and former mining activity are both much in evidence.

CHAPTER 2

Caves, Hominids and the Woolly Rhinoceros: The Palaeolithic

···

We are so accustomed to think of ourselves as islanders that we sometimes tend to forget that Britain is part of the European continent from which she has at certain intervals in her history become temporarily detached. (Grahame Clark 1940, 1)

To understand the evolution of the early landscape of the Clwydian Range, it is important to set the scene and view the area in the context of human development for, as we shall see, north-east Wales and the Clwyds figure prominently in the story of Stone Age Britain and Europe.

The worldwide Palaeolithic context

Human evolution is much more complex than originally thought and whilst the ancestors of *Homo sapiens* go back five or even six million years, actual beginnings go back some seventy million years plus with the emergence of the order of primates. The timescale of human evolution is continually being put back.

There is no archaeological evidence for early man in the Clwydian Range or anywhere else being the club-wielding creature beloved by cartoonists. From an early stage humanity was much more sophisticated. As Gamble (1994) reports, the drawings of early illustrators 'endorsed the sneering assertion of the technological superiority of modern day society over the stone-tools of the past'.

The immediate ancestor of the genus *Homo*, however, was the essentially ape-like *Australopithecus* of some four million plus years ago, bones of which have been found in eastern Africa. Australopithecines could walk upright and *Australopithecus africanus* is thought to be the earliest fossil in the gracile linkage. This links to *Homo habilis* and then *Homo erectus* some two million years ago, a species which spread from eastern and southern Africa to Europe, the Caucasus, China and Java (Taylor 1996, 41). *Home erectus* was probably a recognisable human who walked and looked to a large degree like us and was the first to have lived outside Africa. However, whilst Australopithecines never

FIGURE 12.
The imposing entrance to Ffynnon Beuno Cave, Tremeirchion.

developed a brain much larger than that of a chimpanzee, that of the genus *Homo* developed rapidly.

The European Stone Age

With the above as a basis for thought, what of Europe and Wales? It took *Homo erectus* some 500,000 years to move out of sub-Saharan Africa and how this occurred is hotly contested and unclear, as is the species' ability with language, but it does seem possible that this migration followed that of earlier hyaena and lion movements (Aldhouse-Green 2000, 4, after Kingdon 1993, 2). It could be that either climatic, behavioural or social changes, or the inter-play between man and beast or both, played a part.

As usual with evolution, things are not as clear-cut as we would like, but several species or subspecies of human existed in the period between a million and 150,000 years ago, during which *Homo erectus* and its African form *Homo ergaster* gave way to the emerging *Homo sapiens*. What happened next is the subject of debate. Did anatomically 'modern' humans appear in eastern Africa after about 150,000 years ago or did they appear in Eurasia from this much earlier migrating African source? DNA analysis is beginning to support the 'Out of Africa' theory. Whatever occurred, the earliest evidence in continental Europe for early man is from artefacts. At Soleihac in the Auvergne flakes and pebbles have been dated to 900,000 years ago. Only one specimen of *Homo erectus* has been found in Europe, that of the massive mandible from a gravel pit site at Mauer, near Heidelberg in 1907, possibly as old as 600,000 years.

The discoveries at Boxgrove in West Sussex in 1993–96 of a fragment of shin bone and later two teeth of *Homo heidelbergensis* (a late form of *Homo erectus*) are dated to about 500,000 years ago in the Middle Palaeolithic before the start of the 'Great Ice Age'. They were the earliest evidence of human activity identified in Britain to date, but there is now emerging evidence from Somerset and Norfolk of a date as early as 700,000 years ago (Ashton 2003, 11). Hand-axes and animal bone at Boxgrove indicated that these hunter-gatherers killed and butchered large animals such as rhinoceros and bear.

Life during these times was probably very local and flint tools are indeed rarely found more than 20–30 kilometres away from 'home' territory. Nevertheless evidence is now emerging from Europe that greater movements may have occurred, with stone tools used in the hunting of roaming species, such as red deer and bison, identified up to 300 kilometres from their source (Ashton 2003, 11).

Although Neanderthals were of the same genus as us (*Homo*), some researchers see a different species between *sapiens* (or *Homo sapiens sapiens*) and *Homo neanderthalensis*, whilst others see a *Homo sapiens neanderthalensis* as a subspecies (Taylor 1996, 247–48). Was indeed *sapiens* derived, not from a Neanderthal strain as first thought, but from a distinct type of human that evolved in Eurasia and migrated into Neanderthal domain and ultimately replaced them? But how and when? There is evidence that the Neanderthal physique was itself evolving, and there is the intriguing possibility that Neanderthals perhaps, in some areas, themselves evolved into modern humans on their own, whilst in other areas they were replaced by the early modern humans from either Africa or from somewhere in Europe or Asia or both.

The earliest human skull found in Britain, unearthed at Swanscombe in Kent and dated to about 400,000 years ago, has been interpreted as an early Neanderthal. It is generally considered that Neanderthals *per se* appeared some 250,000 years ago with the 'classic' form about 125,000 years ago. The last evidence for Neanderthals comes from Spain, dated to around 28,000 years ago (Taylor 1996, 108). For tens of thousands of years Neanderthal groups would have roamed as hunters and gatherers over the plains, forests and mountains of Europe, the Near East, Central Asia and possibly as far as Siberia.

The arrival of *homo sapiens* in Europe about 40,000–30,000 years ago at the start of the Upper Palaeolithic and during the middle of the last Ice Age resulted in encroachment into Neanderthal territory. Although these 'early modern humans' were possibly in existence before 100,000 and maybe as early as 150,000 years ago, they had fewer primitive traits and showed the more lightly-built frame of people today. It is possible that their physical distinction from true Neanderthals was not total, but this is a view not accepted by some researchers.

The overlap between Neanderthals and *Homo sapiens sapiens* of several thousand years raises many questions. Was there inter-breeding? Were Neanderthals 'discriminated' against within a 'proto-society'? Why did they remain distinctive until extinction? Were they hunted to extinction by *Homo sapiens sapiens*? Or was their demise the result of something more mundane – disease?

Heidelberg man himself was very robust in stature and that was also the case with the Neanderthals. Heavy, muscular and stocky, with strong brow-ridges and projecting jaw and height of only a little less than that of Europeans today, the unkind image of Neanderthals as the true 'cave men' is still with us. Answers to the above questions are not for us, but consider them as a backdrop to the situation of early man in north Wales from about 250,000 years ago, for Neanderthals will be seen as important to our story of early humans in the Clwydian Range.

Stone Age north Wales and the Clwydian Range

Early humans appeared in north Wales around 225,000 BC, but before we consider the evidence, we need to understand the nature of the climate and landscape in the Clwydian Range and surrounds during the Palaeolithic period, or Old Stone Age, which lasted from about 225,000 to 10,000 BC and which encompassed roughly the late quarter of the Pleistocene Ice Age geological period. Firstly, of course, the climate continually changed, as it has always done and will continue to do. As a result the vegetation and the fauna dependent upon it varied too.

During the glacial periods which we have considered in Chapter 1, great ice sheets covered Britain to varying degrees and, if not covered by ice, the land was perhaps not unlike the Arctic tundra of today, with sea level nearly 100 metres lower than today and with a land-bridge between Britain and Europe. During the warmer interglacial episodes sea levels rose and Britain became an island again. Vegetation changed, woodland increased and animals suited to these more equable conditions flourished.

Britain in fact was never completely covered by ice, there always being areas of the country south of a line from the Severn to the Trent exposed to some degree. As we have seen, in the Clwydian Range things are complicated and we only have evidence for the last glaciation of some 18,000 to 14,000 years ago, with its colder and warmer phases. Evidence in the Clwyds during these colder periods suggests that hyaena, reindeer and bison would have roamed over a treeless tundra-steppe countryside, whilst during the warmer inter-glacials animals such bear, deer, rhinoceros and leopard lived in a wooded landscape. During all of these phases it is likely that extreme cold and ice would have forced groups of people to vacate Britain to more clement areas to the south, only to return at the onset of better conditions, and this could explain the enormous gaps that exist in the archaeological record.

Much of the evidence of early humans has indeed been lost due to glaciation, but 225,000 years ago at Pontnewydd Cave, a short distance to the west of the Clwyds in the Elwy valley near St Asaph, a small group of early Neanderthals lived in an area of open woodland in a good position to observe and track game in the Elwy valley below. The site was excavated by the National Museum of Wales under the direction of Professor Stephen Aldhouse-Green who found the stratigraphy to be complicated by debris-flows slumping into the cave. Here was evidence of warm-climate animals such as wolf, bear, narrow-nose rhinoceros, leopard, roe deer, beaver and species of vole and wood mouse, all suggesting an interglacial period. However, above these layers were the majority of faunal remains and artefacts: hyaena, Merck's rhinoceros, wild cattle/bison, Northern vole and Norway lemming, all colder climate animals, suggesting a later, steppe-type environment. The climate was therefore changing for the worse or at least to a more continental regime (Green 1991, 32–33).

What makes Pontnewydd Cave so special and important to our under-standing of early people in north-east Wales and what puts the Clwydian Range in a wider context, is the finding of human remains. There were 20 such finds from the excavations, representing possibly six individuals and at least two adults and one child (Aldhouse-Green 2000, 18). The mode of depos-ition is uncertain. A range of activities over a considerable period took place in the area manifested by the amount and variety of artefacts found, from cores and flakes suggesting tool manufacture to handaxes, spearpoints, flakes for butchering and scrapers for hide processing.

It was, therefore, during interglacial and interstadial periods that conditions (as today) would have become suitable for human advance. At around 500,000

FIGURE 13.
Cae Gwyn and Ffynnon Beuno Caves, Tremeirchion show the earliest evidence of human activity in the Clwydian Range.

BC, an interstadial period within the Anglian Ice Age would have allowed the hominids of Boxgrove to survive. Likewise at Pontnewydd, a temperate phase, between about 225,000 and 186,000, allowed Neanderthal occupation of the area in an open steppe environment (Aldhouse-Green 2000, 6), and at this time Britain was joined to the continental Europe landmass (Eurasia). For much of the period the Irish Sea, Cardigan Bay and the Bristol Channel were not sea at all, but were wide low-lying areas. Cave sites in north and south Wales were much farther from the sea than they are today. The view to the present Irish Sea from the Clwydian Range at Prestatyn hillside would have been of a wide low plain. Because of the nearness of Pontnewydd to the Clwyds it is compelling to speculate that this small group of Neanderthals may have hunted there; an interesting thought, though there is no evidence.

This is the context for consideration of the Clwydian Range itself, for there is substantial evidence for the existence of early humans here in *later* periods. At The Graig limestone outcrop at Tremeirchion, overlooking a small steep-sided glacial meltwater channel are the cave sites of Cae Gwyn and Ffynnon Beuno (Figure 13). High on the south-facing hillside is Cae Gwyn, suggested by Burnham (1995, 10) as possibly the inner end of a passage which may be a collapsed part of a larger cave. Downslope and showing a most impressive entrance is Ffynnon Beuno (Figure 12). Both have probably been affected by later mining trials and to the east of Cae Gwyn is such a shaft. The two passages do not appear to interconnect despite showing similar sequences of deposits, but this is not clear. In 1885 excavations by Sir William Boyd Dawkins of Manchester University came up with animal bone and stone tools from a wide timespan, greatly mixed together in what was probably a debris flow.

Whether groups of Neanderthals or the new competing *Homo sapiens sapiens* or both were present in the caves has not been determined as no human bone has actually been found, but the stone tools found at Ffynnon Beuno were notable and impressive. They consisted of a large bifacially re-touched leaf point from a possible, but by no means certain, earlier phase of occupation about 36,000 BC, and an Aurignacian engraving tool burin busque leaf point dating from a later phase of about 28,000 to 26,000 BC. The Aurignacian, which has origins in western France, is represented by only a few sites in Britain, all located in the west; Ffynnon Beuno is one of these. Associated perhaps with the latter tool were an angle-burin, two scrapers (re-worked) and a worked bone (Green 1991, 40; Burnham 1995, 11). Finds of tools were not as numerous in Cae Gwyn and comprised a flint blade and a flint end-of-blade scraper. Again, as in Ffynnon Beuno, the stratigraphy proved complicated and as Green (1991, 41) suggests, the archaeological layers at both caves could be complicated because of debris flows which resulted from the great mass of water released by thawing ice or permafrost following the end of the glacial around 13,000 to 8,000 BC.

Hyaena bones predominated in the caves and these animals could have been the main occupants, although other bones showed evidence of gnawing. However, further investigations have come up with a radio-carbon date of a mammoth bone in the deposit at Ffynnon Beuno of about 16,000 BC. Thus, it appears that at the end of the last Devensian glaciation material was deposited by meltwater and, as a result, the stratigraphic sequence in the two caves has been complicated by this glacial deposition.

Another problem is that, except for examples of roe deer which came exclusively from Cae Gwyn, all the animal bones from the two sites were analysed together. The list of species is impressive with over 200 specimens of jaws and teeth of hyaena, but bear, lion and wolf also roamed nearby. Reindeer, woolly rhinoceros and horse were the most prominent herbivores, whilst mammoth and giant and red deer, badger, bovids and wild boar were also found (Green 1991, 44). Ffynnon Beuno was clearly the most productive site for bone (which could indicate debris flow rather than actual usage); but perhaps the type of bone was similar at both sites. No one really knows.

The finds at both caves could, therefore, be a mixture from thousands of years in a final debris flow, but of Early Upper Palaeolithic age. Whatever the case, the work done on the two caves on site is very old and is much in need of further work (Pettitt, pers. comm., 2002). However all of this does indicate human activity in the area. But by whom? Whatever the case, as Professor Stephen Aldhouse-Green (1991, 45) observes, 'Ffynnon Beuno and Cae Gwyn are crucial to our understanding of the spread of upper Palaeolithic hunters arriving, ultimately, from the North European plain'.

Deep in the Carboniferous Limestone of Eryrys Mountain is the sheltered and narrow 'Pot-Hole' valley, the location of the representative site of the Late Upper Palaeolithic period in the Clwydian Range – Lynx Cave. The Cave is sited on a precipitous rock outcrop above the valley and named after evidence of the European Lynx found in later layers. This scheduled site is important and has been the subject of excavation and investigation by John Blore since 1962. Not only is there evidence of early human presence in the Palaeolithic, but also through to Romano-British times.

The findings of the excavations to date are found in the very readable account of the project by Blore (2002). Palaeolithic evidence comes in the form of a single bone, a broken radius from a ten year old female, artefacts and animal remains. Of particular interest was the finding of two separate fragments of possibly a single bone point (maybe an awl or spear) with a radio-carbon date of 11,700 ± 90 BP (OxA–8164), fashioned from the bone of an elk (Figure 14). Elk are still found in parts of Europe today, but no trace has been found of the species in Britain after circa 4,000 BP. The find shows a striking similarity to an implement found in a rock fissure, together with bones of a bear, at Coniston Dib in Yorkshire.

The amount of butchered bone in Lynx Cave was low (Blore 2002, 58) suggesting that either the use of the cave was intermittent or that discarded bone thrown down the mountainside was brought back by carnivores. Two more bones have been radio-carbon dated: a red deer tibia sample to 11,600 BP ± 75 (OxA–7992) and a reindeer sample from the distal humerus of 11,145 BP ± 80 (OxA–7993). A femur of the forest-loving auroch, some 33cm long, found in the Upper Palaeolithic layers, showed signs of shattering at each end when the bone was fresh. It was used to obtain bone marrow. What is noteworthy,

however, is the varied type of animal bone present throughout all of the layers of the cave, not just the Palaeolithic.

Together with bone, 22 flint and chert blades and scrapers have been found. Some are incomplete, the widely held view being that they are of Upper Palaeolithic origin dating from circa 11,000–12,000 BP (Figure 15). Such implements would have been used for cutting and scraping pelts and hides, preparing food and a wide variety of everyday living tasks. As we shall see in later chapters Lynx Cave has more secrets to unveil.

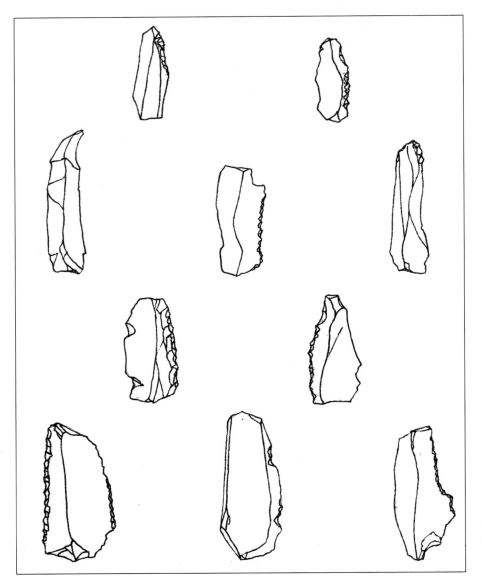

FIGURE 15.
Late Palaeolithic blades and scrapers from Lynx Cave, Eryrys.

JOHN BLORE

CHAPTER 3

The First Land Managers:
The Mesolithic

....

*Change began with the Creation, and ages of momentous
development are shrouded from our eyes. (A. E. Pollard 1912, 8)*

The Flandrian or Holocene interglacial period, within which we now live,
began about 10,000 years ago. There is growing evidence that during the
Mesolithic period, which lasted from about 8,500–4,300 BC, the landscape was
for the first time changed – and indeed managed – by the hunter-gatherer
peoples that lived in it and exploited its resources. These people were modern
humans like ourselves. They were skilled in communication, the use of fire,
and possessed a level of technology which allowed them to alter their surroundings. The Clwydian Range that they would have recognised was an
increasingly afforested landscape.

Landscape and climate

The earliest dated Mesolithic site in Wales is at Nab's Head in Pembrokeshire
with radio-carbon dates of around 9,200 BP (Aldhouse-Green 2000, 23). The
distribution of such sites suggests that Mesolithic people, who were increasing
in number, favoured more open coastal and riverine locations than the people
who came before them.

The climate warmed rapidly after about 10,000 BP, and the landscape was
characterised by birch, juniper and pine vegetation. This Pre-Boreal period
lasted until about 9,300 BP and was followed by another warm episode, the
Early Boreal, which lasted until about 8,200 BP, with birch, pine and hazel
appearing in the pollen record. The Late Boreal phase to about 7,500 BP was
a time of warm and dry climate with oak and elm. Finally the Atlantic phase,
to around 4,500 BP, was a period of oak, elm, lime, ash and alder, the latter
suggesting a much wetter as well as warm climate (Aldhouse-Green 2000, 24,
based on Parker and Chambers 1997).

The Mesolithic was, therefore, a period of marked vegetational change, but
one which opened up new opportunities for an increasingly sophisticated society. The liking of Mesolithic people for coastal and riverine locations does not

mean that uplands such as the Clwydian Range were ignored; they were just exploited differently.

The work of Simmons (1996) on the environmental impact of Mesolithic cultures on the landscape suggests that by 7,000 BP as much as 80 per cent of south Wales was covered by trees. In fact tree growth would have extended to about 700 metres in altitude and, as a result, there would have been relatively little open ground in which to hunt. Deer like a combination of open grassland and afforested areas, as indeed do cattle, and such areas would have been in short supply. Simmons considers that the open shorelines would have provided these Mesolithic hunters with a plentiful supply of raw material for tools, weapons and ammunition and the beaver would have opened up large areas in river valleys, as well as providing both meat and hides.

The relationship between Mesolithic coastal and upland environments has been the focus of many archaeologists' attention, starting with Grahame Clark as long ago as 1972 at Star Carr in Yorkshire. Here he suggested a seasonal movement of red deer between two areas. This is quite possible on a local scale, though the work does not provide an all-encompassing model, but what complicates matters when the present day location of sites are investigated is that often the coast was inland during the Early Mesolithic and many areas favoured by Mesolithic peoples are now under the sea.

Sea-levels and sites in north-east Wales and the Clwydian Range

Ken Brassil (1991, 47), in his analysis of the Clwydian Mesolithic, suggests that during the earlier part of the period the coastline of Britain was very different from today and the English Channel was dry land linked to the continent. The Irish Sea was, in part, an extensive plain, drained by the emerging Dee, Clwyd and Conwy rivers. Subsequently, the melting ice, over a period of only 200 years, resulted in the sea level in this area rising as much as seven metres around 7,000 BC. Great tracts of coastal land, which supported a viable food source, were lost.

The Clwydian Range today directly abuts the narrow coastal plain to its north above Rhyl, Prestatyn and the Point of Ayr. It was, however, much further from the sea when the waters began to rise (Figure 16). This change in land-mass was accompanied by changes in climate, with much warmer, wetter and windier patterns resulting and changes in vegetation to an oak, lime, ash and alder regime in lower-lying areas with moorland dominating the upland tops. There remains much work to be done on these patterns in northeast Wales, but this analysis does set out a possible relationship between the Clwydian Range and the coastal plain.

Manley (1989) suggests that sea level did not rise at a constant rate and that there is evidence of ten major marine transgressions during the 10,000 year period from the Mesolithic to the Medieval period. Thus, for the first two transgressions, which occurred at the start of the Mesolithic, the sea reached as far as Rhuddlan, with a promontory or island of boulder clay at Rhyl surrounded by water. Later transgressions followed a similar pattern. The work of Tooley in north-west England refined this model, defining 24 transgressive and regressive episodes; but generalising we have a rapid rise in sea-level from about 7,000 BC to 4,000 BC, followed by a series of lesser oscillatory movements (Tooley 1985).

The first land managers

The Mesolithic situation in the Clwyds can be gauged by the fortunate fact that three important sites from this period have been identified nearby to the Range: at Prestatyn, Rhuddlan and Tandderwen near Denbigh. Isolated Mesolithic material or evidence has also been found at Splash Point, Rhyl, Ffrith near Prestatyn and Mia Hall near Trelawnyd. Of special interest is the isolated find of a large antler mattock 38cm in length on the shoreline at Splash Point, Rhyl; this has been radio-carbon dated to the fifth millennium BC.

In the Clwydian Range itself there is tentative evidence at Lynx Cave, where two microliths were found, each 13mm in length. They were used to produce a barbed harpoon-type tool (Blore 2000, 60). There is also an isolated find of a worked flint flake, 18mm long, of possible Mesolithic origin, on the north-western slopes of Moel Arthur between Llangwyfan Forest and the hillfort (CPAT 2003). There are also important sites near Llyn Aled Isaf and Llyn Brenig to the west.

There is thus the possibility of people living near to the Clwydian Range and using it as a seasonal hunting resource. In the Berwyn Mountains, a comparable upland area south-west of the Clwyds straddling the Denbighshire/Powys border, people actively 'managed' the vegetation and thereby influenced the landscape within which they lived and hunted. Here woodland clearance may have been the result of Mesolithic hunters creating glades where foraging animals would concentrate and therefore be easier to catch (Brassil 1991, 49). This may have been the situation in the Clwydian Range.

Within sight of the Range, the sites near to the castle at Rhuddlan have been very productive; one site near Ysgol y Castell produced, with burnt hazelnut shells, over 12,000 flakes from sand layers, which could only have been the detritus left from the manufacture of tools from Gronant chert and pebble flint. Although a few worked pieces have been found, including scraper, points and long blades (Brassil 1991, 49), of special interest are pebbles decorated with incised patterns reminiscent of pine needles and possibly a rough representation of a human figure (Miles 1972). These very rare examples of Early Mesolithic art suggests a considerable degree of sophistication.

At another Rhuddlan site, at Hendre, excavations found mainly blades and also microliths. The latter were being prepared for next season's hunting on the hills and scrapers used to prepare arrow-shafts. This evidence represents a renewal of the microlithic component in the archaeological record. There were

no finds to indicate domestic activity, however, and indeed the function of the microliths is itself uncertain (Manley and Healey 1983).

At Hendre, as at other sites, the fine black chert found especially at Gronant and Trelogan on the eastern edge of the Range was used extensively for manufacture. Flint was also obtained locally from the Bunter Beds and overlying drift, or collected from the foreshore. At Hendre, Manley and Healey quote 60 per cent of raw material being of the better quality black chert. Clearly the Clwydian Range and environs was an important source of this raw material.

At Rhuddlan there was a lengthy settlement during both the Early and Late Mesolithic, showing evidence of shelters, postholes and pits. These were possibly bases from which hunters may have sought food over a wide area: from the grazing, shellfish, wildfowl, wild plant and fishing resources of the coast, and from the larger game of the nearby uplands of the Clwydian Range. We can only guess at how these forays took place.

There is further evidence of Mesolithic industry at Prestatyn. A site was found in the 1930s, under tufa/lime deposits directly at the foot of the Clwydian Carboniferous Limestone escarpment and south of the low seaward

FIGURE 16.
The coastal plain north of the Clwydian Range was much more extensive in the Mesolithic.

plain (Clark 1938). A microlithic chipping floor was sealed by the tufa in what were essentially tufa islands within an area of marsh; an inland location well away from the shore at 115–130 metres O.D. on boulder clay. Waterlogged, the site received calcareous-bearing springs gushing out of the limestone, flowing over the impervious boulder clay and precipitating out to form tufa. Similar deposits occur at Caerwys in the Chwiler valley on the south side of the limestone of the Clwyds (see Chapter 4, p. 36).

The Mesolithic finds at Prestatyn indicate substantial activity over a considerable period of time, and indeed later Romano-British graves were also found dug into the boulder clay. As at Hendre the material used to produce Mesolithic tools was locally obtained: dark coloured and lighter grey chert and flint. The list of finds is interesting, for in addition to primary flakes there were many other cores, scrapers and flakes, as well as other items: a perforated oyster shell disc, a pointed bone and an unworked deer tine, hazel-nut shells and red ochre. The microliths were made by the notch method, resulting in the presence of so-called 'micro-burins', which relates this industry to the Tardenoisian period of the Mesolithic; the early phase of the Atlantic period, during which overlying tufa was deposited. Marsh snail shells were also preserved showing that the area was one of wetland pools around a possible hunter-gatherer site.

The earliest evidence of Mesolithic settlement during the post-glacial period, however, comes from near Tandderwen in the Vale of Clwyd. Here temporary lakeside camps for small groups of hunter-gatherers were located on a gravel delta next to Lake Clwyd, near to where the Afon Ystrad now flows into the River Clwyd, and dated to around the fifth millennium BC (Brassil 1991). It is feasible that these camps represent a seasonal migration of peoples from the coastal lowlands up the present Vale of Clwyd to the uplands of the Clwydian Range and Mynydd Hiraethog, in search of game and other sources of food.

During the Late Mesolithic, as rising sea-levels increasingly restricted the narrow coastal belt, there must have been pressure on these communities to make greater use of nearby upland resources as well as the estuarine locations at the mouth of the River Clwyd: hence the importance of sites such as Rhuddlan, from where fish could be caught in summer and wildfowl and game in winter and the resources of the neighbouring uplands also exploited. During the Late Mesolithic in the Clwydian Range, we can hypothesise greater penetration into the uplands in pursuit of herds of red deer in summer and a return to the coast in winter (after Morrison 1980). Such penetration hypotheses have been challenged, and perhaps the pattern of hunting involved the interception of herds' seasonal movements (Manley and Healey 1983), rather than a random pursuit to upland pastures.

Details of the social structure of Mesolithic peoples remains sparse and no evidence has been forthcoming from the Clwydian Range, but at Greasby in Merseyside a structure dating to around 8,000 BC was excavated in 1988, showing a rectangular floor some 21 m square made of sandstone flags and pebbles.

Along its centre would have been three large ridge-poles, some two metres high, which may have supported a tent-like covering of wood or skins. This is perhaps the earliest example of a dwelling in Britain (Dyer 1990, 26), and a similar structure could, conceivably, have been used in the Clwyds.

There is every reason to believe, therefore, that Mesolithic people could well have used the Clwydian Range as a transient or seasonal hunting location, accessed from semi-permanent or permanent bases within striking distance of the uplands. Possible evidence at Lynx Cave and Moel Arthur suggests Mesolithic activity in the area. However, recently these migratory theories have been questioned and it has been suggested that forays into the uplands may have been more to do with 'recreational' activity than hunting. The theory goes that with rising sea levels there would have been increasing pressure on coastal resources, both for living space and food. The inhabitants of these areas would have been put under some stress which would have encouraged them to 'chill out' and relax in adjoining areas (Aldhouse-Green 2000, 41); an interesting thought.

CHAPTER 4

Axes and Agriculture:
The Neolithic

···

> Geography is always a basic fact in human settlement, at any period
> and in any region, but is particularly relevant in a prehistoric con-
> text and in an island situation. (Forde-Johnston 1976, 13)

Evidence of the first European farming communities appeared in Greece in the
middle of the sixth millennium BC and by that time Britain had become an
island with a shoreline similar to that of today. Some 2,000 years later agriculture had spread, via the Danube basin, across the continent to Britain.
These early European farmers grew wheat and barley and kept sheep and
cattle, fished in the rivers and sea and made pottery vessels. Evidence from the
Netherlands and north-western Germany suggests that they constructed long
rectangular timber houses divided into a number of sections, some occupied
by people, some by the animals on which they depended (Dyer 1990).
Whether these people saw an opportunity to colonise parts of Britain, so
bringing their agricultural ideas with them, or whether the later Mesolithic
people crossed to Europe and so brought back to these shores cereals, animals
and agricultural techniques, is hotly debated by archaeologists.

Perhaps both occurred, since there was certainly enough opportunity for
interaction, but radio-carbon dates show that settlements associated with evidence of early farming were established from East Anglia to Scotland from
about 3,000 to 3,500 BC (Darvill 1987, 50). These early farmers would have
been accomplished seafarers, possibly using boats constructed of a
wooden/wicker frame covered with animal skin, akin to the Irish curragh of
today. Sheep, cattle, pigs and goats are not indigenous to Britain and would
have made the sea voyage with their hooves tied together; a technique similar
to that used to ferry animals from the islands off south-west Wales to the
mainland in recent times.

Technological change

Simplistically, the Neolithic can be divided into two distinct phases: an earlier
period (prefaced by a Mesolithic/Neolithic interface around 4,300 BC) from

about 4,200 to 3,200 BC, characterised in Britain by the construction of chambered tombs, earthen long barrows and causewayed enclosures, and a later period from about 3,200 to 2,100 BC characterised by decorated pottery, cursus and henge monuments and smaller long and round barrows. More than at any earlier time, the Neolithic saw profound changes take place in the landscape.

The development of the polished stone axe, so typical of the period, was the instrument by which this change was initially brought about. It made light work of tree-felling, and experiments have shown that a trunk of some 22 cm in diameter could have been felled in half an hour. In 1954 Iverson showed that one hectare of forest could be cleared in five weeks (Dyer 1990, 31). Eight out of a potential 20 sites have been definitely recognised in Britain as axe factories. An important north Wales site was at Mynydd Rhiw on the Llŷn, but the largest in Wales was at Graig Lwyd at Penmaenmawr (Glenn 1935), the impressive headland of augite granopyre on the coast of Gwynedd to the west. Axes worked here found their way into the Clwydian Range (Graig Lwyd axes have been discovered from Dyserth to Llanarmon yn Iâl) and well into the rest of Wales and the north, midlands and south of England (Figure 18). They also form some three-quarters of all north Wales axes found. Although it was used for upwards of 2,000 years, there was little development of the stone axe's design over time. How these vital artefacts were traded is not known, but traded they certainly were and in the Prestatyn area a series of axe finds from a variety of factories could indicate that the area might have been a trading point for export (Houlder 1961).

The cultivation of cleared areas by digging stick and later primitive ard allowed crops to be grown and animals grazed, with eventually an increase in the size of clearings as they were linked by trackways. Tracts of land were thus cleared in linear fashion, and linked by access routes along the 'ridgeways'. It is possible that such an ancient track followed the ridge of the Clwydian Range.

Evidence of Mesolithic activity is characterised, as we have seen, by finds of microliths, points, scrapers and knives, all showing a desire to hunt and skin animals to the exclusion of virtually everything else. Around the mid fifth millennium BC, however, a more sophisticated assemblage of artefacts appears in the archaeological record. This includes querns to grind flour, sickles to cut corn and forage, pottery containers and the polished stone axes. Likewise, major engineering projects appear in the landscape: permanent settlements, large ceremonial monuments and other communal works that would have involved a consumption of energy, an ability to organise events and a management of the landscape that is hard to envisage today.

FIGURE 17.
Gop Cave and Rock
Shelter, Gwaenysgor,
the site of extensive
Neolithic burials.

A more settled way of doing things

A change of emphasis characterises the Neolithic: a shift from the subsistence of individualistic hunter-gatherer societies concerned with satisfying immediate needs, to a reliance on the calendar year to provide sustenance – a harvest of both animals and plants. This harvest requires a lot more than mere individual effort; it requires a sea-change in society towards a communal way of looking at the world. This world view is the basis of agriculture. Undoubtedly this change of emphasis to an agricultural regime was the single most important social transformation that occurred in prehistory.

Such developments would have been gradual, however, probably beginning in the more lower-lying and fertile areas. The break from hunter-gatherer to settled farmer would not have been sharp. Indeed it is not until nearly the middle of the third millennium that evidence of hunter-gatherers disappears from the archaeological record. Most Neolithic people would probably have been seasonally mobile, with shared tenure over pasture and other resources (Barnatt 1998, 93). Later, in upland and western areas in the Later Neolithic and Early Bronze Age, things gradually became more settled and 'permanent' (Barnatt 1996, 54–55).

So what sort of landscape existed at the dawn of agriculture in the late fourth millennium BC? It would certainly have been wooded. Pollen records show that virtually all of Britain was covered by deciduous woodland at the start of the Neolithic and the Clwydian Range would probably have been no exception. The density of the tree growth would be dependent on the nature of the underlying strata and soil type and where the canopy was not as great on the well-drained valley margins, there would have been areas suitable for clearings. In western areas such as the Clwydian Range and in northern Britain generally, birch and pine would have predominated, as opposed to oak, hazel, elm and alder further south. The post-glacial forest still dominated the landscape and determined the type of animals and associated flora present. It is thought that animal species continued to be similar to those of the later Mesolithic, with possibly some decline in red deer herds (Darvill 1987, 49).

Impetus was given to agriculture by a climate that was very favourable to the early farmers. There is evidence that it was better than that of today, with longer growing seasons and less of a need to overwinter animals under-cover. Drought conditions were less and land could be cultivated to higher altitudes.

Evidence of these very early farming communities in national terms is very sparse indeed and, particularly in the coastal fringes which provided food and sustenance to Mesolithic hunter-gatherers, the transition to agriculture from a subsistence lifestyle was no doubt blurred; both could have existed in parallel depending on conditions prevailing at a particular location.

Related to the tufa deposits of the Bryn Newydd Mesolithic site at Prestatyn are extensive deposits of the same material near Caerwys in the Afon Chwiler valley, on the south side of the Carboniferous Limestone outcrop. Here non-marine shells are in abundance and tusks of wild boar, ox teeth and human remains, including a fragmentary skull, have all been found. It has been suggested that these finds are of Early Neolithic date (Clark 1938), though indicating a lifestyle more typical of the Mesolithic period. Whatever was the case the Clwydian Range and environs is fortunate in having some outstanding Neolithic sites.

Cairns and caves

It may come as a surprise that the great cairn at The Gop near Trelawnyd, in the north of the Clwydian Range, is the second largest artificial mound in Britain after Silbury Hill near Avebury (Figure 19, page 42). Although completely overshadowed in the nation's psyche by the latter, it is no less important and no less enigmatic in its origin. Unlike Silbury Hill, which is located on a flat plain, Gop Cairn occupies a prominent hilltop position and it may be that the hilly topography has made people under-appreciate its size. In reality, however, it dominates the Trelawnyd plateau for many miles around and from its summit there are wide-ranging vistas. The site is an oval of about 101 by 78 m, oriented north-west to south-east and 14 m high, built, it seems, of roughly placed limestone blocks with traces of a kerb of drystone walling near and around its base (Burnham 1995, 12). The top is truncated, possibly as a result of the robbing of stone for limestone walls and excavation. In its pristine condition it would have shown a dramatic whiteness set against a blue or darkening sky, in the same way that Silbury Hill would have been of strikingly white chalk.

Gop Cairn has traditionally been assigned to the Bronze Age, but archaeological thought is now tending towards ascribing it, and Silbury Hill, to a Neolithic origin. Lynch (2000, 75) suggests that the cairn may cover a passage grave which can be distinguished from other Neolithic tomb structures, such as portal dolmens (examples of which are in the Conwy valley), rectangular chambers and Cotswold-Severn tombs, by the presence of a well-defined passage-way between the burial chamber itself and the world outside. There is also no forecourt for outside ceremony. Barclodiad y Gawres on Anglesey is a fine example of a decorated cruciform passage grave, comparable with the splendid monuments of the Boyne Valley in Ireland (Powell and Daniel 1956; Eogan 1986).

As Lynch outlines, Barclodiad y Gawres must have been built by people with close links to Ireland, possibly coming to Wales in the Middle Neolithic. It is interesting that the scale of the cairn at The Gop is similar to those on the Boyne and 'much larger than any later monument'. Could there be an Irish connection here also?

But what evidence is there for a Neolithic origin at The Gop? Certainly the monument lies in an area of abundant Neolithic activity and the local name of the site as the 'Hill of the Arrows' because of the large number of arrowheads found there (Glenn 1935, 200), suggests such a date. However, megalithic tombs of that period are notoriously difficult to date and were often used many times over (Lynch 2000). The excavations by Boyd Dawkins in 1886–87 (Boyd Dawkins 1901, 322–41) may give us some clues.

A wide shaft of 1.8 x 1.2 m was sunk into the top of the cairn down to solid rock (met at 7.9 m down) and a drift also dug, 1.8 m high x 1.2 m wide, at the base of the shaft in a north-easterly direction to a length of 9 m. Two other drifts intersected the first one in line of the section. Here Boyd Dawkins found only animal bones of 'hog', sheep or goat and ox or horse, but they were too fragmentary to be determined with certainty. However, the very fact that they were there at all is of interest, especially as he stated that 'they are of the refuse heap type, usually found in prehistoric habitations and burial places'. This suggests that the cairn was sepulchral in function.

With one or two notable exceptions (as with John Blore's work at Lynx Cave) it is unfortunate that virtually all of the cave sites in the Clwydian Range that show archaeological evidence of human activity have either been disturbed – especially in the past 50 years by inexperienced cavers or diggers (Brassil and Guilbert 1982, 4) – or have been the subject of very old excavations which lacked modern dating techniques. As a result artefacts tend to be either in unknown private hands without published description, or indeed lost, and layers irrevocably damaged. In most cases we can only surmise.

Boyd Dawkins' excavations at the Gop Caves show proven Neolithic credentials (Figure 17). He excavated a rock shelter and also a cave in a low limestone cliff 43 m to the south-east of Gop Cairn. Neolithic flint arrowheads have also been found on the hill nearby. Investigations were also undertaken by J. H. Morris in the *inner* North West Cave in 1909–14 and by W. H. Stead and colleagues in 1958. Boyd Dawkins cut into the blocked entrance with two drifts and found a wide rock shelter passing into a narrow passage. The inner cave was found later. He noted four layers of accumulation. A stiff yellow clay floor with no remains was followed by grey clay containing redeposited evidence of 'cave' hyaena, bison, stag, reindeer, roe deer, horse and woolly rhinoceros. There was an indication that antlers of reindeer had been marked by the teeth of hyaena. Above this was a mixed red layer, with flow deposits containing a mixture of refuse and animal bone, whilst higher still charcoal fragments. Pot-boilers for cooking and fragments of pottery increased up the section. The upper layer was 1.2 m thick and showed evidence, according to Boyd Dawkins, of an 'old fireplace' where thick charcoal deposits covered slabs of limestone. He found numerous burnt or broken bones of domestic animals and fragments of coarse pottery. Intermingled with these was a large quantity of human bones of various ages lying under slabs of limestone and forming a continuous packing up to the roof.

Here he made a startling discovery. On removing the remains there appeared a rubble wall regularly built of coarse limestone, which turned out to be the west wall of a rectangular chamber, 'the three outer walls being formed of similar rubble walls, while the fourth was constituted by the inner wall of the cave'. Inside was a mass of human skeletons of some 14 individuals, closely packed together and seemingly interred at successive times. Also found were bowl fragments, a few white quartz pebbles, called by Boyd Dawkins 'luck stones', two links or belt sliders of Kimmeridge shale or jet, and a carefully polished flint flake, the last three in one group. The bodies were crouched, the arms and legs drawn together and folded. In some cases long bones lay parallel to each other. The area of burning described above could possibly be to do with burial ritual and the bodies outside of the chamber indicated use after the chamber was full. In side passages of the adjacent North-West Cave were skeletons of six more people, possibly reinterred from elsewhere.

Links or belt sliders, used as dress fasteners, were found with the burials and date them to the Late Neolithic (Lynch 2000, 75). These are important artefacts, but their whereabouts is now unknown and their exact composition cannot be determined. The overall distribution of links in Britain is sparse with only 23 examples known (Sheridan and Davis 2001, 152) and the find may indicate the wearer's high status in society. Boyd Dawkins observed that the finds were unworn and indeed this is a general feature of belt sliders as a whole, indicating that they were probably a prized possession; a possession to accompany the owner at death. Finds at the cave also include sherds of Peterborough Ware, a flint knife, a leaf-shaped arrowhead and the fine Graig Lwyd stone axe nearly 22 cm long (Figure 18) – all indicating a Neolithic provenance – as well as the lower jaw of a lynx.

To the north-east of Gop Cave is Gop Farm Cave (Gwaenysgor Cave), excavated by Morris in 1910. Morris found human bones and bones of hyaena, woolly rhinoceros, giant deer and Arctic lemming, all indicating a cold

FIGURE 18.
The Graig Lwyd axe from Gop Cave found by Sir William Boyd Dawkins in 1886–87.

climatic regime, as well as flints, again indicating a probable Neolithic presence. As with Silbury Hill, however, the true purpose of Gop Cairn remains a mystery.

Boyd Dawkins was a great investigator of caves and his book *Cave Hunting*, published in 1874, is a classic. As well as at The Gop, he was very active in the Llanarmon yn Iâl area in the south of the Range. Between 1869 and 1872 he excavated the caves at Perthi Chwarae and – nearby to the south – Rhos Ddigre (Dawkins 1874, 152–56), both in the Alun valley. He found, as well as animal bones and flints, communal burials thought to be of Neolithic origin (16 plus at the former and five plus at the latter site, where two of the burials appeared to be in the crouched position). At Rhos Ddigre a Graig Lwyd axe was also discovered as well as pottery fragments.

Other cave and rock shelter sites in the Clwydian Range have also suggested a Neolithic penchant for burial. In the 1950s Stead and Bridgewood investigated the Nant-y-fuach rock shelter, to the south-east of the striking limestone outcrop of Graig Fawr above Dyserth. They found in the shelter the disturbed remains of five persons, inhumed and in a contracted position but without any grave goods (Trump 1957, 219), with fragments of fine gritted and well-baked pottery, a large barbed and tanged arrowhead of black chert with serrated edges in disturbed ground outside (Longworth 1958, 280–81) and animal bones (Chamberlain and Williams 2000). Surface finds in the area of the shelter included some Peterborough Ware, including a cord impressed rim, several stone and flint axes and leaf arrowheads (Lynch 1969, 173), suggestive of Neolithic origin.

To the south of the range in the Loggerheads and Maeshafn area are Ogof Colomendy and Orchid Cave. At Ogof Colomendy investigations in 1975–76 (Davies 1975, 1976, 1977, 1989) yielded evidence of three adult burials with regular fracturing of the long bones, animal bones (ox, red deer, sheep or goat, dog and pig), and leaf-shaped arrowheads and flint flakes of Neolithic origin (Chamberlain and Williams 2000). Human vertebrae, metatarsals, ribs and skull fragments were found with evidence that the bones had been reinterred (Blore 2002, 50).

At Orchid Cave (Brassil and Guilbert 1982, Guilbert 1982a) flint scrapers and animal bones were found with evidence of three or more burials. A radiocarbon date of 4170 bp (OxA–3817) on a human pelvis (Aldhouse-Green, Pettitt and Stringer 1996, 446) firmly indicates Neolithic activity.

All this evidence points to cave burial, with the unburnt remains pushed into restricted crevices with the entrance sealed, being a common practice in the Neolithic. At such sites skeletons are very often incomplete and are a mixture of individuals, a possible indication that they had been exposed elsewhere before being placed in the cave. This process of 'excarnation', still practised in parts of the world today and continuing in Britain in later periods, allows the body to be consumed and to decay naturally, exposed as it is to both animals and the elements. Whether remains were complete and in a crouched position or disarticulated, probably indicates differing burial traditions (Brassil and

Guilbert 1982, 4) at differing times or place; it is quite usual for bones to be deposited in heaps, sorted, arranged and re-arranged over long periods of time and then removed after decay. The movement of bone over time in a burial chamber or cave could just indicate re-use of a tomb rather than excarnation (Taylor 2001, 32). Nevertheless, excarnation was probably the commonest form of disposal of the dead in the Clwydian Range in the Neolithic, followed for the elite few by transference of selected bones to nearby caves and crevices.

What we do not have in the Clwydian Range, however, is the monumental stone tomb and it has been suggested that this tradition did not come to north Wales until late in the Neolithic, and then possibly as a result of the trade in stone axes (Lynch 1986, 19). Tyddyn Bleiddyn is a known Breconshire type chambered tomb in the Elwy valley near St Asaph, whilst Tan-y-coed is possibly another such example in the Dee valley. The portal dolmen became firmly established in the Conwy valley, but just did not become established further to the east in the Clwydian Range.

Sites and summits

Axes were one of the many artefacts found at the sites of King Charles's Bowling Green and Dyserth Castle, in the north of the limestone escarpment of the Clwydian Range and overlooking the flat coastal plain near Gwaenysgor and Dyserth. The former site possibly owes its name to its location on the relatively flat summit of the hill of Bryn Llwyn, or could be a corruption of the Welsh *Bryn Bouling*. This area was clearly one of settlement from at least Atlantic times (Figure 20).

Excavations of both sites took place in the years 1912–14 supervised by T. A. Glenn. On top of King Charles's Bowling Green is a small tumulus dug into by Glenn, who found a cist with cremation burial of probable Bronze Age date (Glenn 1914). Later excavations by T. G. E. Powell in 1951 (Powell 1954), to find specific traces of settlement, discovered only the destroyed tumulus and a worked-over and ploughed surface with traces of charcoal, flint fragments and broken leaf arrowheads.

However, Glenn had been luckier and found a wide variety of flint and stone implements including scrapers, choppers and knives, borers of Neolithic origin and leaf-shaped arrowheads, over 10,000 flint flakes and chips, pottery, a quern-like stone for crushing grain, animal bone (possibly ox, pig, deer, hare and identified sheep or goat) and thousands of small glacial pebbles in heaps – possibly sling stones. Fragments of polished Graig Lwyd axes were found associated with the pottery, which corresponded to the Neolithic floor at Dyserth Castle (Glenn 1935, 191).

On the summit were also found walls of earth and stone but, although Glenn considered these to be of Neolithic origin, they proved to have been much later and probably modern. Despite the lack of an up-to-date interpretation of the archaeology of the site, the artefact evidence suggests that King Charles's Bowling Green had Neolithic settlement of some importance and, as

Powell states, 'the hill seemed to form an important site for cross-channel navigation because of its splendid location'.

Dyserth Castle was erected by Henry III in 1241, but the hill on which it stood has a long history as a settlement site. Excavations by Hughes in 1896 and T. A. Glenn in 1914 (Glenn 1915) outside the castle walls, found abundant evidence of Neolithic activity. Flint, chert and stone implements, leaf arrowheads and some 1,000 flint chips, flakes and splinters indicate that tool manufacture took place here. A possible anvil-stone, a pestle, hammer and grinding stone were also found together with bone/horn implements, part of a bone necklace and pottery fragments. Broken Graig Lwyd axes were found associated with the pottery (Glenn 1935, 192). Bones of horse, ox, sheep or goat, red deer, pig and wild boar and fish, mussel, cockle and oyster shells all suggest that the site was settled to some degree. As we shall see in Chapter 5, there is evidence that this area of Dyserth was also occupied from the Bronze Age through to the Romano-British period and by the time of the building of the castle there had been over 5,000 years of activity at the site.

FIGURE 19. Gop Cairn. The largest man-made cairn in Great Britain after Silbury Hill.

FIGURE 20.
The flat summit of
King Charles's Bowling
Green above the coastal
plain.

The far north of the Range to Prestatyn, Rhyl and Rhuddlan was an area of activity from Mesolithic to Neolithic times and beyond. John Manley (1989, 185) records that around Rhyl alone some 70 prehistoric objects of bone, stone, shell and bronze, of predominantly Neolithic and Bronze Age periods, have been collected from the peat beds and estuarine or marine clays and foreshore. Of course some of these could have been washed up from elsewhere, but they are more likely to suggest settlement nearby and use of the foreshore itself for hunting food and collecting flint and stone, from the Mesolithic onwards. He goes on to suggest that the upper surface of the peat in the bore-holes that have provided evidence for sea-level change in the area, was a land surface of 4,000 to 3,000 BC, 'a time when the Mesolithic economies were becoming increasingly redundant in the face of the new technologies of the first farmers'.

Thus, as Lynch (1969, 173) suggests, despite trading contacts, the Neolithic population of north-east Wales was not affected by the megalithic monument-building traditions of the west. Indeed it is possible that they were the descendents of former Mesolithic populations who had adopted pottery-making and other skills as an outcome of trade and who continued to use caves, especially for burial.

43

What then did the Neolithic inhabitants of the area live in? A clue lies in the excavations by Guilbert (1976) at the Moel y Gaer hillfort near Rhosesmor to the immediate east of the Clwydian Range. He found what appeared to be evidence under the present Iron Age hillfort of a Neolithic long house, similar to that known at other Neolithic sites in Britain and Ireland.

Traces of Neolithic activity are a feature at a variety of Welsh hillforts, but Guilbert's work was important evidence for some form of Neolithic building at such a site. Because of the close proximity of Moel Hiraddug to Dyserth Castle, it is no surprise that the hillfort also shows evidence of Neolithic activity, and it is to this continuum of settlement and use of sites throughout the Clwydian Range over succeeding millennia that we shall return when we look at the Bronze and Iron Ages in the next two chapters.

CHAPTER 5

Weapons and Warriors:
The Bronze Age

I come from battle and conflict
With a shield in my hand;
Broken is the helmet by the pushing of spears.
(Black Book of Carmarthen, poem XXXIII – Squire, undated, 255)

At the end of the Neolithic, around 2100 BC, and into the succeeding Early Bronze Age, the landscape of the Clwydian Range was essentially wooded in character and the climate was drier than today, with fine, long summers. By the Middle Bronze Age, from around 1600 BC, the climate had already begun to deteriorate. These changes were reflected in society and settlement patterns.

Change to both did occur in Wessex and the south-east in particular, where the figure of the Bronze Age warrior forms the atypical representation of the period. There is archaeological evidence for this after about the middle of the third millennium BC, after a long period of what must have been agricultural stability. What came next was tension and in places warfare and, as shown by burial customs, a move towards ranking within society and the emergence of the chieftain. There was also change in the forms of settlement and monument construction, and the vogue for monumental tombs and ancestral cults declined.

Clearance of woodland in some areas may have resulted in soil erosion on sandy soils and resultant social pressure, but there is evidence for a regeneration of woodland in others around the mid-third millennium BC at sites formerly cleared by early farmers. The reasons for these changes are obscure but could have been partly associated with political and ritualistic factors (Darvill 1987, 75, 77). There do appear, however, to have been substantial differences in Bronze Age society between the south-east of England and further north and west into Wales.

As so often in archaeological research, it is to the traditions of burial practice that we must look to glean information about society in general. The Neolithic was dominated by burial in the great chambered tombs and cave burial, as at The Gop, and in Wales as a whole this tradition lasted much longer than in southern England. Generally speaking, there was a substantial

FIGURE 21.
A Bronze Age barrow at St Elmo's Summerhouse, Llanasa in the north of the Clwydian Range.

45

movement away from communal to individual burial in the Bronze Age, with greater inclusion of grave goods (Lynch 2000, 121). Lynch also suggests (2000, 79), that in Wales the 'old traditions were not moribund' and that pressure for change was not as severe.

An example comes from just to the south-east of the Clwydian Range near Mold. Here, beneath a round barrow on the banks of the River Alun, the most important and valuable article of Bronze Age art in Wales, the Mold gold cape, was found in 1833 by quarry workmen. Possibly contemporary with the Acton Park Complex of the Early Bronze Age (Lynch 2000, 102 after Northover 1995, 520), it is indeed one of the treasures of Britain. Of beaten gold and adorned with 300 amber beads, the cape was divided among the finders, and some of the original pieces are still missing. In the 1960s what remained was restored at the British Museum, where it presently resides. Clearly this was a valuable and high status item, but it could not have been used by a warrior in practice as its design restricted the use of the arms. It was, therefore, not for actual use, but probably formed some ritual context in death. That the young man was a sacrificial victim cannot be ruled out.

Urns and uplands

In Wales, as elsewhere, from about the mid-third millennium onwards the round barrow or cairn above cremated bones, often contained in an urn or pot, took over as the principal form of burial. A cairn may cover multiple burials interred at the same time or burials in one mound over a period of time. Alternatively, there may be just a single burial in the centre. Sometimes mounds are placed together in clusters, as at Bryngwyn, Tremeirchion, where five mounds were opened by the Jesuits in the early 1900s. Four contained single burials at the centre, whilst one had secondary burials located at the top (Hubbard 1986, 453). There are many such examples in the Clwydian Range – but why?

In Wales as a whole, and the Clwydian Range is no exception, there is a lack of good agricultural land. The lowland distribution of megalithic tombs in Wales probably suggests that the best land was indeed used in the Neolithic (Lynch 2000, 80). By the Early Bronze Age, however, aided by an increasingly clement climate, there was a movement of agriculture into the more marginal land of the uplands, with a consequent wealth of burial and ceremonial sites found in these areas. The Clwydian Range has the greatest concentration of cairns in north-east Wales. This is especially in evidence on the slopes of Moel Famau; here in a rough triangle bounded by the north-eastward thrusting spur of Coed Cefn-Goleu, the col of Bwlch Pen Barras and the present Offa's Dyke National Trail above the Iron Age hillfort of Moel y Gaer, Llanbedr, are the sites of 17 cairns, though they are now either covered by forest plantation or damaged in some other way.

On Cefn Goleu, which rises to 427 m O.D., M. Bevan-Evans and P. Hayes excavated two sites between 1950 and 1954 in advance of forestry operations

FIGURE 22.
The enigmatic Clwydian landscape near the important Bronze Age cairn sites of Cefn Goleu and surrounds, Moel Famau. Moel y Gaer hillfort, seen in summer here and in winter in Figure 30, dominates this landscape.

(Bevan-Evans and Hayes 1952–53, 1954–55). Nearby they found evidence of two structures. It is quite possible that Moel Famau, the highest hill in the Clwyds, with its striking summit dominating the landscape for miles around, held some ritual significance. This would have been a mystical and powerful landscape with far-reaching vistas in which to bury the dead (Figure 22).

The first and much disturbed cairn excavated was recorded by Canon Ellis Davies in the nineteenth century and is worthy of special note. It was 12.8 m in diameter and 1.1 m high, with remnants of a surrounding stone-ring or kerb and a long 'boat-shaped' central cist-grave (the primary burial), with blackening by smoke around the grave area. There were no bones and it was filled with rubble. To the edge of the grave to the south was a large stone slab; beneath it was a layer of grey clay and then another slab under which was

found a secondary cremation burial, 'enclosed in a leather bag', consisting of fragmentary burnt bones, burnt shale, charcoal, a charred mature hazel-nut and small pieces of worked flint. The bones were those of a small child plus some sheep and lamb. The remains of ten other secondary cremations were found under the cairn, placed in two distinct groups to the south and east of the central grave, making twelve burials in all, some in urns (Figure 23).

It is tempting to make a connection between the primary burial and secondary burial, the latter as either an early age death or sacrifice, but in the absence of more modern analysis this can only, like the date, be conjecture. Whilst Bevan-Evans and Hayes point out that the method of construction of the cist-grave of packing stones in an upright position to form the sides was of well-known construction in the Neolithic and Early Bronze Age, they also indicate that Glyn Daniel dated the grave to 1500–1000 BC.

Cremation 8 is most interesting, consisting of an overhanging-rim urn containing a miniature urn or 'pigmy cup', of which some 50 examples have been found in Wales of varying styles, size and crudeness of form. Here the large urn, which was placed inverted in a 33 cm deep pit, contained cremated bones of a young adult, probably female, of about 18 to 25 years of age. Her teeth had been worn down, possibly by eating gritty food. The pigmy urn was placed, mouth upwards, in the larger urn, to one side of the centre and embedded in calcined bones. In it were the broken-up bones of a very young infant, together with some cremated adult bones (clavicle, rib, long bone), part of a human finger, four fragments of a bone pin, charcoal and fire-reddened

FIGURE 23.
The Bronze Age Cefn Goleu urns, Moel Famau.

mudstone. According to the excavators there can be little doubt that this young woman died in childbirth and ash and bone were placed in the two urns. However, this finding is exceptional and it is generally thought that the meaning of pigmy cups is unknown, although Lynch (2000, 128) suggests that their presence could indicate some formal and complex ritual involved in the funeral proceedings.

Other cremations in the cairn produced complex burial sequences, but the differences in sequence of burial at each point are striking; no two are alike. Some have urns, some not; some are beneath slabs, some not. Grave goods were few, with some evidence of bronze and bone pins and in one a barbed flint arrowhead and the tip of another, scrapers and a possible knife fragment. High infant mortality is indicated by three young children of under six months of age, whilst teeth problems were suggested; one adult displayed evidence of abcess formation with absorption of the bone. There was a wide variety also in the pottery forms of the urns and these variations suggest that more than one social group could have been involved.

But where did the people who buried their dead in such a place live? Bevan-Evans and Hayes suggest that in a small valley near Bwlch Pen Barras there is possible evidence of two hut circles. One hut was partially excavated and proved to be a regular circle of dry-stone walling 5.2 m in diameter with walls two courses high and about 1.1 m in breadth, making a three-metre interior. No artefacts were found and its dating and use is open to conjecture as it could be much later.

A second much-disturbed cairn was opened some 1,280 m to the south of the Cefn Goleu cairn at around the same altitude, near Bwlch Pen Barras. Called the 'Nursery Cairn', it was smaller in diameter at 7 m and had a considerable quantity of white quartz pebbles in the inner part, with a stone ring sunk to the west to take account of the sloping ground. It is probable that a large central pit contained a primary burial. The site is interesting in that it is virtually identical in location to the Cefn Goleu cairn on top of a ridge running east to west, giving an extensive view to the north-east and south. The location, together with the stone ring and central grave, point to similarities between the two sites and they could, therefore, both have witnessed similar rituals and cultural practices (Bevan-Evans and Hayes 1954–55, 139).

Whatever the date of the sites, the general upland nature of Bronze Age cairns in Wales indicates the exploitation and settlement of areas which must have been far more hospitable in the Bronze Age than they are now. The Coed Clwyd area of Moel Famau was especially favoured as a burial place. On the opposite side of Bwlch Pen Barras on the Moel Fenlli summit there is another mound and nearby to the south on the level top of a narrow ridge at Moel Eithinen there are several turf-covered barrows, one 14 m across. All are located to make best use of their outstanding positions. Among many others in the high Clwyds are, to the north, cairns at Bwlch y Parc and between Moel Llanfair and Moel Plas. Lynch (1991, 70) indicates that there is a record of another cemetery mound at Llanarmon yn Iâl.

There are cairns at lower levels in the Range, some also in magnificent hill-top positions as at St Elmo's Summerhouse, Gwaenysgor (Figure 21). There are likewise notable clusters in the Trelawnyd/Cwm/Tremeirchion/Dyserth area. At Cwm, for example, there are groups around the pass above the village, one being excavated where an urn with cremated bones was found (Hubbard 1986, 341).

These upland burial sites may have been connected to the increasing use of the uplands for agriculture. Since tribal groupings of the later prehistoric and historic periods began to evolve during the Bronze Age, their prominent positions may represent territories occupied by separate tribal or family groups (CPAT 2003). The sites of many cairns are also close to prominent passes through the Range, perhaps, we may conjecture, because of some ritual associated with burial practice.

There is undated evidence that caves were also in use in the Bronze Age Clwyds for the deposit of human bone. Blore (2002, 51, 60–61) suggests, on artefact evidence, that the remains of some seven individuals were reinterred at Lynx Cave in a mound at the back of the cave. A bronze pin of possible Bronze Age date was also found (Figure 24). Radio-carbon dating is required on these layers. There is also an indication that the Nant-y-fuach Rock Shelter at Dyserth may have had Bronze Age connotations (Chamberlain and Williams 2000).

Circles and stones

A feature of the Bronze Age is the stone or banked circle and although examples occur above Llangollen to the south and on Mynydd Hiraethog to the

FIGURE 24.
A Bronze Age pin from Lynx Cave, Eryrys.
JOHN BLORE

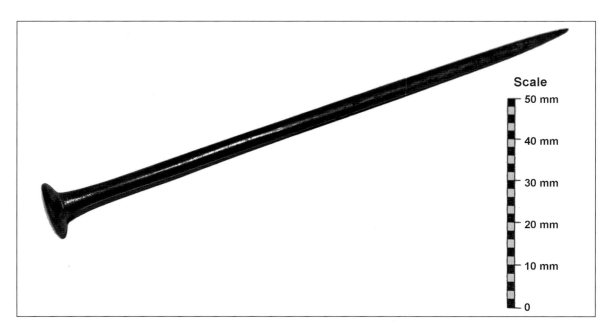

Scale
- 50 mm
- 40 mm
- 30 mm
- 20 mm
- 10 mm
- 0

west, the only possible example in the Clwydian Range is the circle on the Penbedw estate near Nannerch (Figure 25). There is some question about its authenticity, as it is not located in an ideal site for such a feature, although only 500 m away from a genuine round barrow which was opened in 1860 to reveal charcoal, ashes, calcined bone and pot fragments with a zig-zag pattern (Davies 1949). There are five stones in the circle at Penbedw remaining, with six oak trees planted to complete the circumference and a single pointer/outlying stone 250 m due west of the main circle. The largest stone remaining is 1.5 m in height and one metre across. Burl (2000) concludes, with reservations, that the circle is maybe a fake and it is significant that early writers, such as the antiquary Edward Lhuyd, who knew the owner of the estate and with whom he corresponded, do not mention the circle. Nevertheless, if not part of antiquity, it is now very much a part of the heritage and history of Nannerch and its landscape.

Lynch (1991, 74), however, suggests that the single standing stone was a 'preferred ritual monument' in north-east Clwyd and especially in the Alun valley. A worthwhile explanation for the erection of these memorials remains elusive despite some excavation elsewhere; although she does state that deposits of pottery could indicate a Bronze Age date. Much more research is required before we can come to any conclusions.

Hoards and trade

Bronze in prehistory was an alloy of copper (90 per cent) and tin (10 per cent) and the origins of metal-working in Britain go back to the third millennium BC. Metal prestige goods from the continent found their way into the graves of the wealthy in southern England, but in Wales it is the more mundane tools that predominate in the archaeological record.

There is evidence that trade and exchange took place with the continent and with Ireland. The emergence of a warrior elite or aristocracy gave impetus to weapon manufacture which, with tool production, expanded greatly (Needham *et al.* 1989). In 1962, as a result of a small landslip, 'on the sloping ground in the southern part of the enclosure' of the Moel Arthur hillfort, a hoard of three flat bronze axes was found. All had a strong green patina and showed evidence of use and date to the Early Bronze Age. They were remarkably similar in size, varying from 16.5 to 15.6 cm in length and 9.4 to 10 cm in width (Forde Johnston 1964a). The copper contained significant amounts of antimony and came from a single copper source in Ireland; the axes were imports from there. This find is the most important of its kind in Wales and indicates the importance of the Irish industry to metal-working at the time (Figure 26).

FIGURE 26.
The Bronze Age hoard of bronze Irish flat axes from the slopes of Moel Arthur hillfort.

THE MANCHESTER MUSEUM, UNIVERSITY OF MANCHESTER

In the Late Bronze Age, from about 1100 to 600 BC, burial practice in a generalised British context appears to have changed again. Urn cemeteries progressively vanished and burial and ceremonial monuments declined in numbers. By about 1000 BC, many of the traditional practices had declined, although flat cremation cemeteries do occur to the end of the period. An increase in high-status metal objects found in river, bog and marsh contexts is coincidental with this decline. These finds in rivers may simply have been votive offerings, or they could in some incidences indicate a change in burial tradition, with, for the warrior aristocracy at least, the scattering of ashes in water. It is likely, however, that for the mass of the population, as in the Neolithic, excarnation would have been the primary means of disposal.

The deposition of metal objects as hoards *per se* also increased in quantity and intensity during the Late Bronze Age; a hoard being defined as the 'deposition of objects together in one circumstance and placed as a deliberate act'. The result may be that objects were just hidden for safety, with the possibility of recovery, or deposited as an act of ritual or propitiation.

Hoards come in all shapes and sizes, from a small group of objects left under a rock on a personal basis, to a whole series of items, possibly broken, which may have been discarded by a merchant or manufacturer (scrap hoards), or items deliberately disfigured and bent as a deliberate act of sacrifice to the gods, often in a watery context. The famous hoard found just outside the Gaer Fawr hillfort at Guilsfield in the Severn valley in Montgomeryshire (Davies 1967), with its hundred or so broken pieces and unsuccessful casting, is probably scrap. However, the hoard at Broadward in Shropshire containing swords and spearheads (Burgess, Coombs and Davies 1972), and that at Llyn Fawr in Glamorgan, with cauldrons and Hallstatt sword among other pieces, possibly indicate a ritual context through to the Iron Age.

To the west of the Clwydian Range near Abergele, at Parc-y-meirch at the foot of the crags beneath Dinorben hillfort, archaeologists have found a bronze harness and jangles, the earliest evidence in Wales of the use of the horse as a status-enhancing symbol. This find has been dated to around 900 BC, some 200 years earlier than the Llyn Fawr hoard. Later at Llyn Fawr, bronze cheek pieces from a horse-bit and other harness items indicate the increasing importance of the horse in society, a trend which reached its zenith in the succeeding Iron Age.

In the Clwydian Range itself, the axe hoard from Moel Arthur has already been mentioned. On a natural rock ledge of the west-facing limestone outcrop of Craig-yr-Wolf near Eryrys in the heart of the Range, a hoard of gold and bronze objects was found by a geology student in the early 1980s. This was an important find as the gold items were all placed within the socket of a facetted bronze axe (Figure 27).

Green (1982, 15; 1984) describes the objects in detail. The gold consisted of two bracelets, separately and tightly coiled into small spirals, and a piece of a small gold link in place on one of the bracelets, together with a second joining piece of the same link and a small gold ingot, which could have been

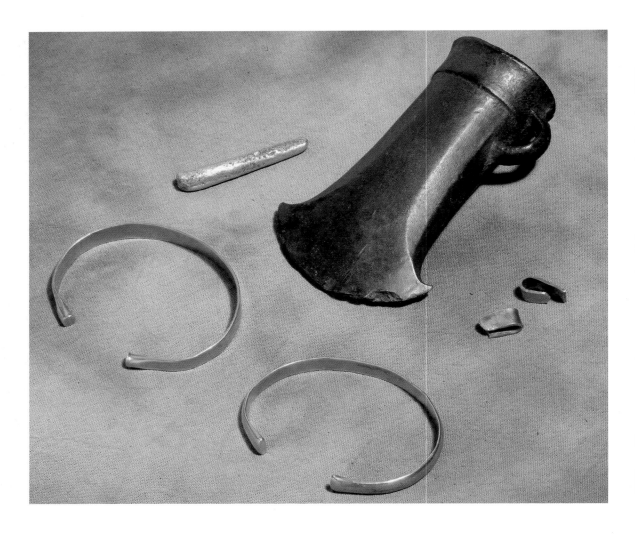

melted down from a bracelet. The bracelets were composed of 78.4 per cent and 79.7 per cent pure gold, with silver and copper, and are typical of western European gold of the Late Bronze Age. This inclusion of around five per cent copper as an alloy in the gold is also typical of gold-working in Britain and Ireland at the time, but the inclusion of silver to a high content (between 14.5 per cent and 19.8 per cent) indicates a possible Welsh source for the gold. The bronze axe has parallels with the Gillespie type, indicating that it dates from the Ewart Park phase of the Late Bronze Age, circa 900 to 700 BC, and metallurgical analysis of the bracelets supports this interpretation. An Irish origin was most likely for the metal of the axe, again indicating the importance of the Irish connection in the Bronze Age Clwydian Range.

It is clear that north-east Wales had become a link in the trade of Irish and European decorative gold and bronze metalwork by the Late Bronze Age. The hoard of gold torcs (from the latin *torquis* – a twisted necklace, wreath or collar) and armlets found in 1782 at Coed Bedw on the northerly lower slopes

FIGURE 27.
The impressive Bronze Age Craig-yr-wolf hoard, Eryrys, of gold bracelets and facetted bronze axe.

of Moel y Parc above the Afon Chwiler, and the heavy gold torc found nearby at Bryn Sion near Ysceifiog, are all likely to have come from Ireland.

It is unfortunate that the Coed Bedw hoard was found in less enlightened times as it was sold and melted down. It consisted of what was thought to be a casket at the time, but was possibly a staved bucket or cauldron with bronze mounts which fell to pieces when dug up. In it, however, were 'seven armlets of twisted of wreathed gold fastened by hooks in the manner of torques [torcs], four additional and heavier torcs, a large piece of solid gold with ring attached and a large gold chain with beads about the size of pigeon[s'] eggs with a ring between each'. A Middle to Late Bronze Age date was later placed on the items by Sir Cyril Fox (Davies 1949, 431–32). In all, the items made up 5.44 kg of gold in weight. If the hoard had not been destroyed it would clearly have been as important a Bronze Age gold hoard as any found in the British Isles.

Fortunately, the Bryn Sion torc has suffered a kinder fate. It was initially found in 1816 in a small limestone quarry, possibly associated with a nearby and lost cairn at Bryn Sion Bach Farm, where it was cast aside as a piece of iron and later used as a hoop to keep a gate closed. Bought eventually by the Duke of Westminster, it is nearly 36cm in diameter and just over 127cm in length, weighing 737g. The single bar of gold had been beaten into four flanges and then twisted into a spiral and was given a Middle Bronze Age date of around 1200 BC. It is considered to be an example of Irish smiths emulating Near Eastern techniques. A heavy bronze looped and ribbed palstave was also thought by Miss Chitty to have been found around 1865 in the vicinity of Bryn Sion (Davies 1949, 423–427) and is now in Shrewsbury Museum (Figure 28a).

Trade was evidently taking place between Wales and Ireland during the Bronze Age as the flat axes from Moel Arthur have already shown, but the

FIGURE 28A.
Bronze palstave from Ysceifiog found circa 1865 in the area of the Bryn Sion gold torque.
SHREWSBURY MUSEUMS SERVICE

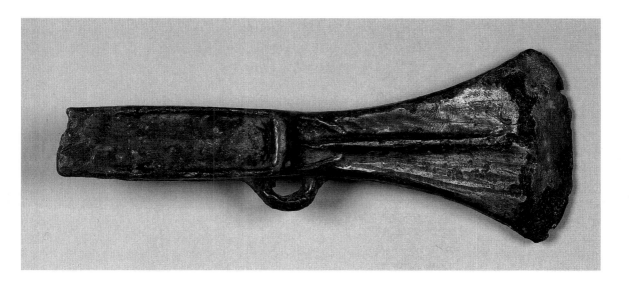

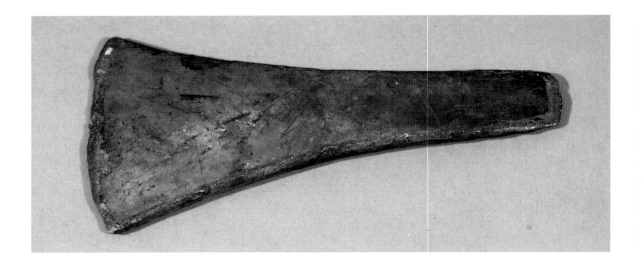

magnificence and evident worth of the Coed Bedw hoard, the Bryn Sion torc, the Mold cape and the Craig-yr-Wolf hoard from a few miles away do indicate substantial wealth in the area throughout the Bronze Age.

Another hoard found later at Gwernymynyd near Mold, contained pal-staves, socketed axes and a bronze mould for a socketed axe (Grenter 1989), whilst the bronze flat axe shown in Figure 28b came from Llanarmon yn Iâl. In the Clwyd area, later Bronze Age tools are generally found in the lower river valleys, whilst weaponry of the period tends to be found in moorland and wet-ter peaty contexts (Lynch 1991, 78), more indicative of a votive context. Weaponry becomes more common as time progresses.

Climate and change: towards the Iron Age

Around 1800 BC the warm period which began in the Neolithic (when the cli-mate was more like southern France is today) slowly began to deteriorate. From about 1400 BC this trend got progressively worse, the climate getting cooler and wetter until the end of the period, about 700 to 500 BC, when things got a little better. The upland areas would have experienced this cli-matic worsening more deeply. In these regions of Wales, Scotland, Ireland and England, where woodland had been cleared, soil denudation would have occurred as a result of intensive farming practices and water-tables would have altered for the worse.

The effects of bad farming practice and a worsening climate contributed to large areas being turned into heath, moor, bog and marsh. By 1400 BC the soils of the North Yorkshire Moors, settled only a few hundred years before, were already in a poor state (Hutton 1991, 134). The uplands of Wales and Ireland and much of the higher land of southern Britain and marginal lands of the east assumed their 'present' appearance at this time. The Clwydian Range was no exception.

No doubt other factors were involved and in 1159 BC the eruption of an Icelandic volcano badly affected northern Scotland and may have played a part in altering weather patterns further south. At this time the erection of ceremonial monuments – so numerous before – virtually ceased in the upland areas. The lack of worthwhile dating evidence in the Clwydian Range precludes any detailed hypothesis, but on what is available so far this scenario could also have been the case here. The process of change was gradual, over hundreds rather than tens of years, and we know its effect on the landscape must have been profound, though a great deal more work has to be done before we can consider the process in detail.

It is unfortunate that Bronze Age settlement has left so few traces in Wales and in the very Early Bronze Age there is virtually no evidence available at all. The most complete indication of settlement is in fact in the far south-west of Wales at Stackpole Warren in Pembrokeshire which shows activity through the Iron Age and into the Roman period (Benson *et al.* 1990).

As a result, it is to the Clwydian Range hillforts, which we will be encountering in the next chapter, that we will be looking to give us some indication of continuity of settlement pattern from the Bronze Age into the succeeding Iron Age.

CHAPTER 6

Nothing Is What It Seems:
The Iron Age

Lug cut off Balor's head, and though Balor had bidden him set it
on his own head so that he should gain its power he set it on a
pillar-stone. Its venom split the stone into four pieces.
(Rees and Rees 1961, 37, after Cath Muighe Tuireadh,
ed. B. O. Ciuv 1945, Dublin)

The nature of Iron Age social structure has generated much heated debate in
academia, as has the impact of Iron Age society on landscapes that are still
very much alive today. There is no real agreement as to when the Iron Age
began; estimates vary between about 800 and 600 BC. Nor can anybody be
exact as to when it ended, as things coalesced into what is generally called the
Romano-British or Romano-Celtic period, dating from the Roman conquest
of AD 43 to about AD 450.

There is also uncertainty as to the climate and vegetation changes which
occurred at this time. The Blytt-Sernander scheme of climatic sub-division,
where the start of the Iron Age corresponds to the beginning of the cool and
wet Sub-Atlantic period, does not correspond with the dating of detailed
vegetational change represented by pollen and macro-fossil data (Briffa and
Atkinson 1997, 98).

A problem in Wales is that there are few Iron Age pollen sequences to assess
vegetational and climatic change and landscape character; there are in fact
none at all from the Clwydian Range. The nearest is from Cefn Mawr on
Mynydd Hiraethog to the west of the Clwyds (Jenkins, Lacelles and Williams
1995). Here peat deposits indicate a reduction in woodland in the Middle
Bronze Age, with replacement by grassland. Woodland further declined from
the Late Bronze Age, with the landscape remaining open through the Iron
Age. To the south, at the Breiddin hillfort north of Welshpool, woodland
clearance began in the latter half of the Bronze Age and continued into the
Early Iron Age.

It seems from these and from other sites in north-west and south Wales,
that areas began to be cleared of woodland during the Bronze Age, with evidence from the south of increasing tree cover in the Iron Age, possibly

reflecting a decline in agriculture as in southern England. Renewed clearance began in the Late Iron Age and Roman periods, seemingly a reflection of a greater demand for pasture (Dark 2000, 67–68).

Certainly the Iron Age was a period of great change in the landscape and environment of Wales, and in upland areas, such as the Clwydian Range, woodland removal might have begun later than on the more hospitable lower ground. Whatever the facts are, it is likely that the landscape was more wooded than today.

At a social level it appears that the Iron Age was an insecure time in which to live. If you were a member of the elite it had its compensations; if you were not. your life was nasty, brutish and short. However, the Iron Age was also a period of development: of trade, power-politics and great art. Dichotomies characterised the Iron Age: in material culture, in structures such as the great hillforts; and in the ritual, religion and myth which permeated society. Things were not as they seemed to be.

The Celtic debate

The Celts have become synonymous with the Iron Age, but there is considerable debate as to whether 'Celt' is indeed the correct name for those who lived at this time in the lands north of the Mediterranean, as far as the British Isles. Did the Celts actually exist or is the term unhelpful? Was the real situation a pattern of widely differing local and regional autonomous groups of people as Collis (1996) and James (1999) infer? There is so much political capital involved in the 'Celtic industry' that to question it is fraught with danger. So let us try to disentangle things and apply them to society in the Clwydian Range during this most exciting time. There are two ways of looking at the problem: what we will call, purely for the sake of argument, an 'heroic' view and an 'insular' view.

An 'heroic' view of Iron Age society

The difference in considering this period from earlier times is that we have some written (if embellished) evidence on which to base our judgements. Material comes from four sources: the classical Greek and Roman authors, who discussed the Celts in a biased way; the post-Roman Irish and, to a lesser extent, Welsh literary sources and laws; archaeological evidence; and finally from comparative knowledge of past and present societies.

The Greeks first referred to the Celts, using the term *keltoi*. With the exception of a specific Spanish tribe, it was an all-encompassing term. Certainly the actual people did not think of themselves as 'Celts', and the classical sources recognised them by their way of life, political organisation and appearance and not by their name. Likewise 'Celt' was never applied, *per se*, to the people of Britain, but strictly speaking to a single Gaulish tribe; but we shall use the term nevertheless.

How did Celtic society develop? It is now accepted that Iron Age society *evolved* in Britain out of a Bronze Age farming society, as a result of continental contact over a longer period, rather than as a result of an influx of continental invaders. This evolutionary process would have been especially true in peripheral regions such as Wales, where the evidence points to a continuum from previous times.

Where did all of this begin? Two main European cultures had an impact on Bronze Age Britain. The first – though it is not now universally recognised as purely Celtic – was the Iron Age Hallstatt culture, of which there is scant evidence in Wales apart from finds at the wetland site of Llyn Fawr in Glamorgan. Named after a rich grave site in Austria, the Hallstatt is characterised by wagon burials dating from about 700 to 500 BC. The second, definitive of Celtic society, was the La Tène, from about 500 BC to the Roman conquest, out of which a rich and characteristic Celtic art evolved. At La Tène, a votive site on the banks of Lake Neuchâtel in Switzerland, fine decorated sword scabbards and related material were found in 1857. Exploration continuing spasmodically till 1917 (Cunliffe 1997, 31).

Celtic society was established in Britain by 600 BC. One hypothesis is that it continued to flourish for nearly a century and more after Julius Caesar's campaigns of 55 and 54 BC, the beginning of the increasing influence of Rome. Society evolved as a hybrid Romano-Celtic or Romano-British culture, during which some of the most outstanding achievements were in Celtic art, of which there are outstanding examples from the Clwydian Range. Much also depended on location, for the Romans had greater influence in what was later to become England than they did elsewhere in the British Isles.

From the first century BC classical writers such as Strabo, Tacitus, Poseidonius, Lucan and Caesar began to consider Britain and refer to the names of client kings of Rome and tribes. The Deceangli inhabited north-east Wales, including the Clwydian Range. Although at the time of Caesar the classical accounts relate to the continental Celts rather than to the people of Britain, an heroic view of Iron Age society would argue that, in general terms, there were similarities in social structure on either side of the channel.

What we do know is that Iron Age society was entirely oral in tradition, and it was not until the eighth century AD, at the earliest, that things were written down in the Irish and, to a lesser extent, the Welsh vernacular texts. These writings, which centre around myth and legend, reflect an archaic society that was formerly thought to exist in Ireland and Wales, but is one that modern scholars have used as a model for pre-Roman Britain as a whole, as in the writings of Ross (1998). The Irish texts show a pagan society, differing somewhat from the Welsh literary tradition where the clerics responsible for putting the stories down in writing tended to 'Christianise' events. What is important is to see these sources for what they are: the past set down in myth and legend as an example to the present.

The Irish (Brehon) and Welsh law tracts, likewise, give a valuable insight into how Celtic society was organised and go back to about the seventh century AD in their written form. Welsh law was heavily influenced by Roman legal norms, whereas the Irish had a more ancient tradition; both were probably handed down in verse form. The Irish law tracts, in particular, deal with a society that has resonances with that described by the classical authors, and archaeological evidence tends to back up the view of an essentially aristocratic society (Ross 1998, 35).

What emerges from the Irish legends is an heroic society of Iron Age warriors, head-hunting, cattle raiding and chariots in battle, the most famous and longest of these being the Táin bó Cuailnge (Cattle Raid of Cooley), itself part of a longer series of stories known as the Ulster Cycle The hero of the story, Cú Chulainn, undertakes heroic deeds, beheading the three terrifying sons of Nechta Scéne. The number three and the mythological significance that three embodies was important to Iron Age society, as we shall see in the Clwydian Range.

The Irish texts put kings at the top of the social order and below them nobles, who were also warriors and owed obligations to their king. Below still were venerated and skilled men including the druids, bards and craftsmen. Beneath them were varying degrees of freemen, mostly farmers; then bondmen in the service of their social superiors and finally slaves. Metal 'parade gear' in the form of sword pieces and the magnificent shield boss from Moel Hiraddug hillfort in the north of the Range (Figure 36, page 82), together with evidence of sling stones at Moel y Gaer, Rhosesmor hillfort to the east of the Clwyds, all indicate a warlike and possibly 'martial' society in the Clwydian Range at some stage during the Iron Age.

In continental Europe evidence of Celtic society tends to follow similar lines, reflected in the classical texts. Here society was also tribal and power-oriented and based on the family, with chiefs and warriors held together by bonds of personal loyalty and cemented together by favours and rewards. Activity was centered around the feast, where champions, deeds of valour and bravery were venerated. Caesar noted that the Celts were organised into three social orders: *druides*, *equites* and *plebs*; translated as 'learned men', 'warriors' or 'nobles' and the 'ordinary people'.

The king and nobles formed a warrior caste whose power and prestige depended upon martial prowess and their ability to attract dependants because of success in raids and minor warfare. The more successful a warrior was, the more retainers he could attract and so on. The ruling aristocracy was thus competitive and status conscious, with power dependent upon the amount of land, the number of cattle and number of dependants it controlled. The latter could be free landowners tied to those above by systems of contractual relationship or 'clientage', which also linked the ranks of the nobility themselves in a system of mutual largesse. This system is dealt with in great detail in the Irish laws. Likewise, the division of the father's estate after death between his sons contributed to the competitive accumulation of wealth and the distribution of this largesse. A system of this sort existed in Denbighshire until the thirteenth century, and in most of the rest of Wales until the Acts of Union in the sixteenth.

FIGURE 29.
Moel Fenlli hillfort,
located above Bwlch
Pen Barras and the
Vale of Clwyd, shows
activity from the
Bronze Age to Roman
times.

Plunder, especially of cattle, could also provide a practical outlet to what Celtic warriors enjoyed doing best: fighting and feasting. Having fought, the 'champion', whose role was the embodiment of power in Celtic society, was given the honour of carving meat for others and in this process gave himself the best bit or 'hero's portion'. This Celtic love of feasting is mentioned by the Greek writer Poseidonius, who described heroes as: 'moved by chance remarks to wordy disputes . . . boasters and threateners and given to bombastic self-dramatisation'.

These ideas are attractive and there is plenty of evidence from across Britain – some of it from the Clwydian Range – to suggest that the heroic explanation of Iron Age society is appropriate. What we can be sure about, however, is that these were times of considerable trade, with exchange underpinning the power system. In Britain social structures were unstable, with raiding and warfare important activities, and with the control of others a cornerstone of society. This was reflected in the building of hillforts, so much a feature of the Clwydian landscape today. However, there is another and less exciting view of what might have occurred. What follows is adapted from James (1999).

An 'insular' view of Iron Age society

At the end of the Bronze Age and into the Early Iron Age a farming-based society existed and hillforts, earthworks and rounded buildings and associated material culture developed in a continuum with what had gone before: some hillforts of north-east Wales and the Marches (including probable examples in the Clwydian Range) have Bronze Age origins (Figure 29). Things were organised on a local basis and kinship groups formed the main social structure. Everything was small-scale but inherently unstable, as personified by the use and disuse of hillforts throughout the 'hillfort zone' That is not to say that people were completely isolated; for example salt containers from Droitwich in the English Midlands are found in Welsh Marches hillforts. Continental and Irish contact also occurred and it was this contact that enabled new thoughts and ideas, for example designs for metalwork, to be taken up throughout Britain. As Jope (2000, 3) observes: 'it seems now clear that there is little biologically heritable basis for the notion 'Celtic'.

Before the Middle Iron Age there is little evidence of a social hierarchy or of classes of people as detailed in the classical and Irish texts. There are few signs of a warrior aristocracy or of a priesthood early on; warfare and religion were not just the preserve of an elite few. Only later did personal adornment become more marked.

From the third century BC, however, new patterns emerged. Agriculture became more intense and field systems and settlements developed. Querns and quernstones for grinding flour have been found at Moel Hiraddug and at the former Dinorben hillfort near Abergele; metal tools for agricultural use have also been found at the latter. In some areas hillforts declined. Roman imperial expansion brought greater continental influences to Britain even before the conquest in 43 AD. From the fourth century BC fine examples of La Tène Celtic art appears similar to those found on the continent: torcs, weapons, horse and chariot trappings and equipment for the feast. Some individual burials appear and there seems to be a move towards the individual *per se*, with a growing sense of social identification. However, the differences with continental examples are so great as to imply an insular pattern to contact, with ideas rather than people arriving in Britain.

It is perhaps at this point that the two hypotheses tend to converge to a degree in that, after the Middle Iron Age, the appearance of La Tène finery does indicate a self-appointed superior class developing in society, with possible warrior or heroic ideas and beliefs, and with a greater degree of ceremonial in religious matters. Things would still have been locally based, however, as the variation between artistic design shows. In the later Iron Age and the Roman period 'tribal' groupings developed, not as a result of mass identity but more to satisfy the aspirations of empire-building dynasties.

Much hinges on how the evidence is interpreted and, therefore, how society developed in the Clwydian Range is open to conjecture. We shall never know exactly, but we do have models to go on and there is much work to be done, not the least in the function and purpose of the great hillforts of the Clwydian Range. But first we need to examine the possible worldview of the people themselves.

Superstition and the gods

The people of the Iron Age Clwydian Range would have been intensely super-stitious and everyday life would have been controlled by the gods. There is plenty of evidence for this elsewhere (Cunliffe 1991; 1993; 1995; 1997; Green 1986). The gods would have been manifested in the coming and going of the seasons, in the ever changing weather, in good harvests and bad, in success or failure, famine or plenty. The notable festivals throughout the year – *Imbolc, Beltaine, Lughnasa* and *Samain* – assumed great importance. Gods would be present in the earth, the sky, water and fire and would have to be pleased, placated and feared. At the heart of this connection between celestial and worldly events were the priestly class, synonymous with Wales – the Druids.

That the Druids existed as a class of society in prehistory is without ques-tion; what we do not know is how they permeated society at the local level, in places such as the Clwydian Range. There is plenty of evidence that north Wales, and particularly Anglesey, was a stronghold of Druidic power and Druidic rites appear, as we shall see, to the east in Cheshire. This power would no doubt have affected the Clwydian Range also. We can only say that we have an overall model to go on.

According to Strabo there were three classes 'held in special honour': the Bards (*bardoi*) were the singers and poets with proficiency with the lyre – pos-sible parts of a lyre have been found at Dinorben; the Vates (*ouateis*) interpreted sacrifices, and the Druids themselves were concerned both with natural phenomena and with moral philosophy. Other classical authors attrib-ute slightly different interpretations, but on a similar theme. According to the Welsh texts the situation was slightly different, there being grades of learned men. At the top were the Druids who are hardly mentioned in the records, but the various classes of poet formed the cornerstone of the king's court. Above all the poet's praises and songs sustained the king in his kingship, but his satire could strike the king from his realm (Rees and Rees 1961, 17, 181).

A great deal of power lay in Druidic hands, and was consolidated by their manipulation of ritual. They officiated at the worship of the gods and con-trolled sacrifices – sometimes human sacrifices. There is growing evidence for this practice. One of the preserved bodies found at Lindow Moss in Cheshire had been pole-axed, garrotted and had his throat cut. His stomach contained mistletoe, a plant traditionally associated with the Druids, and he could have been a Druidic sacrifice.

The object of sacrifice appears to be one of divination: the Celts being much concerned with good and bad days and times for doing particular things. Thus, writhings during the victim's death-throes would be interpreted by the Druidic priest one way or another and then acted upon by the tribe. Pliny describes how the Druids: 'prepare a ritual sacrifice and feast under the tree, and lead up two white bulls whose horns are bound for the first time on this occasion. A priest attired in a white vestment ascends the tree and with a golden pruning-hook cuts the mistletoe which is caught in a white cloth'. Such men held overwhelming power in such a superstitious society and their power could have held sway in the Iron Age Clwyds.

As the supernatural was a part of everyday life in the Iron Age, ritual was seen as a necessary precursor to everything. Sacred places, where man and god could communicate, were a necessary part of the scene. The classical author Lucan describes: 'many dark springs running there, and grim-faced figures of gods uncouthly hewn by the axe from the untrimmed tree-trunk, rotted to whiteness'. When the Roman army was campaigning through north Wales in AD 59, one of the last strongholds of the Druids on Anglesey was attacked and destroyed and Tacitus describes the Roman soldiers as 'hacking down the groves, sacred to savage rites and drenched with the blood of prisoners': all good biased stuff with, no doubt, an element of truth.

Woodland locations were but one setting for Celtic ritual and rocks, ancient trees, springs, bogs and river confluences could all be inhabited by a deity. As in the Bronze Age, there is ample evidence of ritual offerings in watery contexts and some of the finest works of Celtic art have been preserved in this way; for example the votive offerings found in Llyn Cerrig Bach on Anglesey. The impact of the ever changing landscape of the high Clwydians can be imagined.

No real evidence of actual shrines or religious structures of the period have been found in Wales earlier than the Romano-British/Roman periods, although temple sites at Caerwent and Lydney could have Iron Age origins. In north Wales there is some aerial photograph evidence suggesting a ditched enclosure with traces of a possible temple building in the Vale of Clwyd near Ruthin. Below Pen y Corddyn hillfort near Abergele, at Llys Awel, a statuette of Mercury (the Roman messenger god), images of dogs and a few Roman coins have parallels with offerings made at Lydney and indicate a shrine (Green and Howell 2000, 68; Blockley 1991, 126–127). Evidence of ritualistic activity may also come from part of a possible Romano-British or later ceremonial bronze wand or sceptre from Dinorben; this may be a priestly emblem. But, alas, there is nothing of this nature yet from the Clwydian Range.

Superstition and ritual are evident in the design of everyday objects, such as drinking vessels. Beer and mead figured prominently and a love of feasting accounted for a variety of works of art. A beautiful firedog of the late first century BC/first century AD comes from Capel Garmon near Betws y Coed. It would have been used to contain the fire and is associated with the roasting of meat. It has stylised horse or bull motifs to the terminals. Both animals were venerated in Celtic society and it is possibly an example of 'deliberately ambiguous, zoomorphic symbolism' (Green 1992, 222).

A feature of Celtic art is that things are not what they seem and in the above case the power of two animals is represented as one. The yew stave tankard with bronze covering and elaborate handle with broken-backed scrolls from Trawsfynnyd in Gwynedd, also found in a bog, is clearly for the feast. The late first century AD bronze bovine-headed escutcheons, from a wooden bronze sheet-covered vessel found at Dinorben in 1912 and 1956, are also notable examples.

This ornamentation could have imbued the contents of the vessels with mystical power and has resonances in other examples of Celtic art from the Clwydian Range itself, as we shall see at Moel Hiraddug. Cattle were a measure of wealth in Iron Age society in both Britain and Ireland and there is no reason to believe that, with the above evidence from nearby, this was not also the case in the Clwyds.

Symbolism was also evident in personal adornment In the twelfth century Gwalchmai ap Meilyr, the warrior-poet of north Wales, wrote in *Gwalchmai's Gifts*:

> Fearless in battle with my golden torque,
> A lion in the first rank of the host
> Am I ...

Although medieval in origin, these lines hark back to earlier heroic times of the Celtic warrior resplendent in golden torc, fearless, often naked, and ready for battle. This is the picture that has come down to us, displayed in all its true splendour in the famous Hellenistic statue of the 'Dying Gaul' of around 240 to 230 BC, originally erected by Attalos I of Pergamon in celebration of his victory over the Gauls. The torc, of which the examples from Snettisham in Norfolk from around the time of Caesar's conquest are as fine as any, was worn around the neck and it would have blessed the wearer with not only a symbol of wealth and status, but also with mystical properties and divine protection. The Late Bronze Age gold torc found at Bryn Scion and those from Coed Bedw, Ysceifiog have been mentioned above. No doubt the torc was a venerated possession in the Clwydian Range and its environs in prehistory.

There is evidence, both in Britain and Gaul, of the cult of the human head and the ritual collection of heads as trophies, whereby the new owner became embued with the spirit of the vanquished. At Dinorben, the finding of fragments of human skulls could indicate such a practice in north-east Wales. Certainly Iron Age people's attitude to the dead was very different from ours. The finding of inhumation burials at Moel Hiraddug and Dinorben hillforts does indicate that the dead were in close association with the living and there are widespread occurrences throughout hillforts in Britain of burials below the floors of roundhouses or nearby outside. The ancestors were quite literally part of people's lives.

What then did the Iron Age people of the Clwyds look like? A lot is said in the classical texts about this and the Irish sources seem to back up these observations of a people with a distinctive appearance. Diodorus Siculus and Strabo mention their hair and the custom of washing it with lime-wash and drawing it back to the nape of the neck, not unlike a racing cyclist helmet of today: 'for the hair is so thickened by this treatment that it differs in no way from a horse's mane' Celtic coins depict the Celtic warrior on his chariot with two prancing horses, his long stiff locks streaming behind him.

Of course, in such divergent societies there would have been a mixture of types and of all colours, but the blond Celt, strong of frame, appears to have been the ideal for both men and women that the classical authors referred to. Dio Cassius, the Roman author, refers to Boudicca, Queen of the Iceni of East Anglia as: 'huge of frame and terrifying of aspect'. The small dark Celt, of which Cú Chulainn was one, is also of popular tradition and maybe more applicable to the inhabitants of Wales at the time. The Celts were, therefore, seemingly obsessed with their appearance and loved personal ornament and decoration, including tattoos. The brooch and pin finds from Moel Hiraddug and Dinorben testify to this. Woad has healing properties and its use in body decoration could have also had a medicinal purpose to a Celtic warrior.

The best of the Roman cavalry was recruited from the Celtic tribes and their prowess with the horse, both in Gaul and Britain, is referred to in the texts. The picture of the mobile Celtic chariot pulled by two draught-ponies is a feature of many a school textbook and often depicted on Celtic coins. Chariot and horse-harness fittings have been found at Moel Hiraddug (Figure 35, page 80) and Dinorben as well as Llyn Cerrig Bach, so perhaps the classical and Irish writers were correct after all.

In dress the Celtic tribes also appear distinctive and the finding of spindle whorls for winding wool at many Iron Age hillfort sites (including Moel Hiraddug and Dinorben), indicate that the production of cloth was an important activity. Ross (1998, 46) details the type of dress that would be worn by Celtic peoples. Trousers appear to be the everyday wear for men, emanating on the continent from contact with horse-riding peoples, such as the warlike Iranians and Scythians. A knee-length tunic might be worn, with elaborate woven designs, caught at the waist by a belt (iron buckles have been found at Dinorben), or a girdle with a cloak fastened by a brooch. Brooches themselves could be very elaborate and decorated with coral or tufa, as in those found at Moel Hiraddug, or be more utilitarian, as in the iron and bronze examples of penannular brooches found at Dinorben. The Irish texts say that women also wore tunics, but to the ground, with cloaks, brooches and other adornments. Two spiral bronze finger-rings have been found at Dinorben and another from the later prehistoric level at Dyserth Castle.

The Celtic cloak was famous and heavily taxed in the Roman period and in its colourful and exotic form displayed the power and status of its wearer. The cloaks of the Irish kings are well described in the texts and details of weaving and dyeing can be found in the Irish law tracts. Ross (1998, 48) quotes Strabo in his famous comment about the Celts of Gaul, which may or may not be appropriate to those in Britain:

To the frankness and high-spiritedness of their temperament must be added the traits of childish boastfulness and love of decoration. They wear ornaments of gold, torques on their necks, and bracelets on their arms and wrists, while people of high rank wear dyed garments besprinkled with gold. It is this vanity which makes them unbearable in victory and so completely downcast in defeat.

In all of this, the utilitarian objects found in a wide variety of hillfort and other contexts demonstrate the importance of personal appearance to these Celtic peoples. A hand mirror from Birdlip in Gloucestershire and in north Wales tweezers and a possible Early Iron Age razor from Dinorben, are examples of this fastidiousness.

It cannot be said, of course, that *all* of the above would have been applicable to *all* of the people *all* of the time, and it must be remembered that a lot of the writing of the classical authors was about selected tribes of Gaul, who were undoubtedly much richer than those occupying the hillforts of the Clwydian Range. However, there is enough iconographic and archaeological evidence to suggest that we do have, as Ross puts it 'a widespread (and) general mode of clothing' in evidence. Theories concerning the physical appearance of such people and the nature of the society within which they lived also have to be taken seriously.

The hillforts of the Clwydian Range

The most visible and impressive of all the archaeological sites in the Clwydian Range are the Iron Age hillforts that adorn the tops of the hills along virtually all its length. All that is left today are remains of earthen or stone ramparts, ditches and hut platforms. The ramparts, when complete, were probably surmounted by timber palisades with complex entrances and great gateways and possibly with flanking 'guard chambers', whilst the ditches would have been deep and potentially unscalable. When fully occupied, they must have been an awesome sight and would have been visible for miles around.

Hillforts occur throughout Wales and southern Scotland and in a zone extending down the west Midlands to Wessex and south-west England. There are six hillfort sites in the Clwydian Range, all of substantial size, and they must have held an important status in a society where the main living accommodation was the farmstead or the small, defended enclosure at lower altitude. Whilst hillforts must have served some defensive function, it is likely that they also had a psychological purpose as a means of intimidation and coercion. They enabled local potentates or communities to control access to territory, farmland, trade and natural resources, and to display their presence; in this respect they had a similar purpose to the medieval castles built in later centuries. Power and control of the landscape were the watchwords of the day.

Certainly farming would have provided the mainstay of Iron Age society and much work is required to investigate the relationship between lower-lying areas and the hillforts on the tops. For example, a series of possible prehistoric enclosures have been found on the western slopes of the Range at an altitude of 250–300 metres, close to a stream or spring and near to a pass and midway between the Vale of Clwyd and the hillforts above. It is possible that these were linked in some way and may have been for stock management. Alternatively they could be of Bronze Age origin (Clwyd County Council 1995). Increasingly, with the greater use and sophistication of archaeological techniques, smaller farmsteads and defended enclosures, with their characteristic roundhouses, are being found in major river valleys such as the Severn and much work has to be done on this aspect of Iron Age life in the environs of the Clwydian Range.

Moel Fenlli

Among which the highest is Moil Enlli on the top whereof I saw a war-like fense with trench and vampier, also a little fountaine of cleere water'. (Camden 1600)

Moel Fenlli hill takes its name from the Benlli the Giant (*Benlli Gawr*) who, according to legend, was lord of Iâl in the mid fifth century AD. The summit hillfort at 511 metres O.D. covers 10 hectares and controls Bwlch Pen Barras, one of the main passes through the Clwydian Range, overlooking the Vale of Clwyd. Its site is strategic in being directly above the col, with the Vale of Clwyd stretching to the west and the pass through the Range to the east – a similar arrangement to the siting of Moel Arthur to the north (Figure 29, page 62).

The location of the fort is no accident. This is a large site surrounded by very steeply sloping land on three of its sides to the west, south and north and has a summit a bit like a dome. It has been suggested by Burnham (1995, 60) that the present pathway up and along the side of the hill to the in-turned banked entrance to the west is the original one, suggested by Forde Johnston (1964b, 2) as being on this side to ease access to the vale. As at the Penycloddiau hillfort to the north, at first sight Moel Fenlli appears to be a typical contour fort – but it is not, the eastern end being considerably higher than the west. The ramparts are at their strongest where they cross the summit of the hill, with two banks and ditches with a counterscarp bank and an inner quarry ditch. Unlike many hillforts in Wales, Moel Fenlli has a water-source in its interior. Throughout the high Clwydian Range springs are fairly common and characterised by patches of 'flush' vegetation (Brown, Ratcliffe and Hawkes 1980).

There is ample evidence of hut platforms on the site and these can be seen despite the heather. On the highest point of Moel Fenlli are the remains of a Bronze Age cairn of about 30 m in circumference. Interest in the site predated the hillfort.

W. Wynne Ffoulkes and the Rev. J. Williams undertook eight days of 'excavation' in 1846 and the north-west entrance still shows evidence of this disturbance (Wynne Ffoulkes 1850; Davies 1929, 184). Remarkably, these old excavations were published in the journals of the local historical and

antiquarian societies of the time. At Moel Fenlli it was found that the track-way had an 'artificial surface at the entrance formed with stones of some size, laid flat-ways as a rude pavement': an important find. Likewise, the southern entrance was found not to be original, for 'it was found to pass over the original agger, which had been apparently been levelled for it'. Subsequently the ramparts to the south were sectioned at various points. Pottery was found, some certainly Roman Samian and other red, black and cream-coloured ware. A 'remarkable stone knife' could have been a hone according to Davies. Corroded iron, glass, a 'leaden' ornament and a 'bronze' ring together with flint arrowheads were also turned up.

As we have seen in Chapter 5, the area of Bwlch Pen Barras was important in prehistory. A chance find in 1804 of a large black polished stone hammer or anvil stone, at the Pass on a pile of stones, was reported by Davies (1929, 190). It was referred to by Sir John Evans in his book *Ancient Stone Implements, Weapons and Ornaments of Great Britain* of 1872. Interest in the site continued in later centuries: two Roman coin and ceramic hoards were also found at Moel Fenlli and Bwlch Pen Barras. Pennant (1781, 26) called the latter *Bwlch Agricola*.

Moel y Gaer, Llanbedr

> Moel Gaer, a small hill under Moel Venlli, is also strongly fortified with a single dyke, which entirely surrounds its summit: this appears to have been an outwork to the camp or principal station of Venlli. Immediately above Moel Gaer is Moel Vamma. (S. Lewis 1842)

Of all the hillforts of the Clwydian Range Moel y Gaer, Llanbedr is the most curious in terms of its site. It is the lowest in altitude and unlike all the others (Figure 30). With Moel Fenlli, the site commands the pass of Bwlch Pen Barras, this time from the north, but unlike the more prominent hilltop positions of the other five forts in the Range, it is located on a spur jutting out into the Vale of Clwyd from the massif. Whether Moel y Gaer was an 'outwork' of Moel Fenlli has not been the subject of investigation. Slopes are very steep to the west, north and south and the site has double ramparts on these sides, but on the less steep eastern approach there are three. Tellingly the site is overlooked in its entirety on this eastern side and, despite these extra defences, this side would have been vulnerable to observation and attack, suggesting that hillfort location wasn't only about defence.

There are two entrances to the north-east and west. The western one is simply through the outer bank, with an in-turned passage through the inner rampart, but the north-eastern entrance is more complicated, a dog-leg from the outer through to the main rampart which is protected by in-turned ends. No other hillfort in the Clwydian Range has this ingenious device, which would result in attackers 'running the gauntlet' through the defences. There is no water on the site and no traces of hut platforms. An outermost rampart was inadvertently destroyed by agricultural operations in the 1980s.

FIGURE 30.
Moel y Gaer, Llanbedr hillfort. Its unusual siting, in being overlooked from slopes above, makes it one of the most interesting sites in the Clwydian Range.

In 1849 W. Wynne Ffoulkes carried out a similar eight days' 'excavation', as at Moel Fenlli (Wynne Ffoulkes 1850). A number of sections were opened, revealing at the north-east entrance in the inner rampart a 'rude sort of pavement formed with large flat stones, varying in size from 6 to 12 inches long': i.e. a paved entrance. On the north-west side of the outer rampart beneath the surface was found 'a quantity of stone roughly laid together, forming a sort of wall, which, in the centre of the agger (rampart), is carried down to the foundation': this was probably a stone rampart, and there are references elsewhere to evidence of stone being cut from the rock. According to Willoughby Gardner (1926) the second ditch and slope are set with a *chevaux de frise* (sharp stones set at angles) to discourage any attacker, but this awaits excavation. Finds were confined to a few pieces of glazed red Roman pottery.

It is the reference, however, to areas of burnt stone and oak being found that is of special interest, for it possibly tells us of a catastrophic event that befell the hillfort. At the inner rampart, northwards from the north-eastern gate, Wynne Ffoulkes found 'debris of soil and splintered rock-stone so thoroughly burnt as to look, when fresh turned up, like brick-earth'. The burnt oak and stone indicates that the fort could have been subjected to a fire at some point and it appears that this involved a palisade or timber structure on top of the rampart. Such fires, whether accidental or not, did occur on hillfort sites and Ffridd Faldwyn at Montgomery shows evidence of vitrification (O'Neil 1942).

Davies (1929) describes nineteenth-century finds from Moel y Gaer, now long lost, but of passing interest nevertheless if they indeed came from the hillfort. There were two bronze 'implements': a palstave with loop, and an 'axe', which were shown at the Ruthin meeting of the Cambrian Archaeological Association in 1854. They could have been of Bronze Age origin which, if so, would have told us a great deal about the site. Again in passing, Davies cites the finding of a circular stone hammer at Llanbedr and three spindle whorls at two sites nearby, one of which was used as a 'roller or caster to a bed' – such were the uses to which heritage was put in the Victorian period. Moel y Gaer, Llanbedr, despite its less imposing presence when compared with other hillforts in the Range, has many secrets to give up and would repay further investigation.

Moel Arthur

> On one of the summits of the mountain, at a great height above the house (Penbedw), is a very strong British post, with two ditches of prodigious depth, with suitable dikes on the accessible sides: and on that which is accessible is a smooth terrace levelled along the hill, probably a place for exercising the possessors. This post is called Moel Arthur, perhaps in honor of our celebrated prince (Pennant 1781, 60).

Moel Arthur contrasts with Moel y Gaer, Llanbedr in occupying a very strong defensive position on the summit of the Range at 440 m O.D. It directly commands the col of another of the main passes through the hills at Bwlch y Frainc, in a similar situation to Moel Fenlli at Bwlch Pen Barras. The hillfort is, therefore, sited to control access through the Range from east to west – this is a strategic hillfort location *par excellence* (Figure 31, page 74).

The site is roughly circular at 5 ha, and sits on top of the hill to look like a monk's tonsure. The ramparts are strongest and double with strong banks and ditches along the less steep northern side and at the eastern end of this is an entrance. An inner quarry ditch runs around the whole circuit of the hill-fort, located inside the multiple ramparts of the north side. As at Maiden Castle, Bickerton, a Marcher hillfort in Cheshire (Varley 1935, 1936), the outer rampart is higher than the inner. The entrance is in-turned and the in-turns curved in claw-like fashion, with guard-chambers (Forde Johnston 1964, 18). Guard chambers are a feature of many hillforts in the Welsh Marches and allow the entrance to be protected on either side before the gate is reached. There are hut circles in the interior.

The site was part-investigated by W. Wynne Ffoulkes in 1849 (Wynne Ffoulkes 1850; Davies 1949, 269). Near the western extremity of the inner ram-part pieces of red Roman pottery, flint fragments and corroded iron were found, but to the south of the entrance, alongside the rampart, were two stone 'pieces'. The largest, of four metres, was rounded at each end and over two metres thick. The second, somewhat smaller, was nearby. Ashes and flint fragments were found amongst the soil around the stones. This unresolved find needs modern investigation to determine its exact nature; a possible votive or religious significance could perhaps be considered for this immensely inhospitable and exposed site.

Last century a possible Mesolithic flint was also found nearby, as outlined in Chapter 3, whilst the hillfort itself may well be of Bronze Age origin, in common with other sites in the Range and Dinorben and Pen y Corddyn to the west.

The Bronze Age hoard of three early flat axes found at Moel Arthur has been mentioned, but why were such valuable and life-preserving tools left deliberately? It could be that the site had ritualistic significance and that the person who deposited the axes was making some statement or offering. Perhaps the very nature of the site, being located at a high altitude, was closer to the gods of the sky. High altitude sacrifices – of valued possessions or even of people – often indicate that a site held special significance.

Penycloddiau

The northern-most hillfort of the high Clwydians is Penycloddiau. At 21 ha in area and 440 m O.D. at its highest point, it is one of the largest and most impressive hillforts in Wales (Figure 32, page 75). Like Moel Fenlli and Moel Arthur the site dominates one of the main passes through the Clwydian Range; this time from present day Nannerch to Llangwyfan and the Vale of Clwyd. As with Moel Fenlli and Moel y Gaer, Llanbedr, Penycloddiau and Moel Arthur are easily seen from each other; an interesting observation in itself.

FIGURE 32.
The ramparts of
Penycloddiau hillfort.
At 21 hectares one of
the largest and
impressive sites in
Wales.

FIGURE 31 (*opposite*).
Moel Arthur hillfort
occupies a fine strategic
position to control
access through the
Clwydian Range.

At first sight the hillfort appears simple in form, with a single rampart following the contours at the southern end and with an outer ditch, a counterscarp bank and an inner quarry ditch. However, its architecture is in fact much more complicated. As at Moel Fenlli and Caer Caradoc near Clun in Shropshire, a section of the ramparts crosses the contours; at Penycloddiau they cross the top of the hill at the northern end taking in the highest point, with quadruple banks and ditches at this most vulnerable point. The fourth bank is separated from the other three by a berm of about six metres in width and the ditch outside the fourth bank could be unfinished.

Ford Johnston (1964, 20) suggested that rather than the whole fort following the contours, this skewed site allowed greater accessibility via a south-westerly spur to the Vale of Clwyd below. The southern entrance is not as simple as it first appears and is sited further down the hill than it might have been. It is flanked by in-turned banks, the in-turns of unequal length as at Castell Cawr, Abergele, with a possible single guard chamber inside the entrance. East of the southern entrance the ground slopes steeply away and the fort is univallate to meet an in-turned eastern entrance, reminiscent of the entrances at Moel Arthur and Moel y Gaer, Bodfari (Hubbard 1986, 403), but with additional curving hornwork on the south side and no guard chambers.

This is a complicated fort which uses its superb natural setting of slope and crags and rock outcrop to great effect. To the north the ramparts are largely of stone and towards the southern end the quarry ditch has been cut out of the rock – no mean feat. As a result of a heather burn in 1962, a series of hut emplacements were noticed close to the north-east bank (Burnham 1995, 58). Davies (1949, 273) records that in 1925 a flint scraper and several other flints were found on the site and observes that Lewis (1842) states that 'in the centre of the camp is a large tumulus', and indeed a 'mound' is marked on the 1914 Ordnance Survey map. Like the majority of the Clwydian Range hillforts, a Bronze Age origin might also be the case at Penycloddiau, with even earlier interest possible. The whole site merits further investigation.

Moel y Gaer, Bodfari

South East and by south of Potuarry on the great hill there is a moniment of a huge trenche ... (Edward Owen, late sixteenth century)

At 206 m O.D., Moel y Gaer, Bodfari is the lowest in altitude of the Clwydian Range hillforts, but this is only a matter of topography as the site is impressive and the defences formidable (Figure 33). Multiple ramparts, where necessary, make full use of the natural slopes which are precipitous to the east and south-west and very steep to the west. The north is less well protected, but the entrance here, again making full use of natural drops, is awkward to get through. The gap through the inner rampart is similar to that at Moel Arthur in having a T-shaped arrangement which, with a nearby sharp drop, only allows access via a narrow path.

Students of nearby St Beuno's College investigated the site in 1908 and made ten 'cuttings' near to the ditches (Davies 1949, 39). On the west side, the ditch was V-shaped and a two-metre-thick layer of charcoal was found, the possible vestiges of a fire. In the charcoal layer there was part of a deer antler and a water-worn haematite pebble; haematite was mined nearby in the nineteenth century. No traces of structures were found and in contrast to the other Clwydian forts, there were no Roman finds. Other excavations revealed some evidence of the structure of the ramparts. Davies (1949, 41) also refers to chance finds of two flints in 1911. Whether Moel y Gaer has Bronze Age origins has yet to be determined, but the fact that the Coed Bedw hoard and Bryn Sion torc were found only a short distance up the valley from the fort, does suggest that this area was an important centre of activity in prehistory.

It is the magnificent strategic location of the site that strikes the observer immediately: it lies directly above where the valley of the Afon Chwiler opens out to the Vale of Clwyd. The hillfort, therefore, directly controls this major routeway through the Clwydian Range; the major road and former rail route of modern times. Lewis (1842) had similar ideas:

FIGURE 33.
Moel y Gaer, Bodfari
hillfort controls the
entrance to the Afon
Chwiler valley from the
Vale of Clwyd.

To the east of the village [Bodfari] is Moel y Gaer or the 'Hill of the Camp', apparently a British work, and probably constructed for the purpose of defending the pass through the Clwydian mountains.

The fort also directly overlooks the confluence of the Chwiler and Clwyd. Confluence locations themselves may have had considerable mystical significance to the Iron Age inhabitants of the Clwydian Range of some 2,500 years ago. The gods would have been thought to live at such locations; they were places where it was advantageous to be and to make offerings. The site of Moel y Gaer Bodfari may have been selected with spiritual purposes in mind.

Moel Hiraddug

Moel Hiraddug was quite simply the most magnificent hillfort in the Clwydian Range – *was*, unfortunately, because about one-third, the northern end, has been entirely destroyed by quarrying, a fate that befell Dinorben and Penmaenmawr in their entirety. However, rescue excavations at Moel Hiraddug between 1960 and 1980 by a variety of researchers and later by Ken

FIGURE 34.
Moel Hiraddug hillfort
above the coastal plain.
Formerly the greatest of
all the Clwydian
hillforts, now part-
destroyed by quarrying.

IAN BROWN

Brassil and colleagues (Brassil *et al.* 1982) have revealed much of the character of the place and managed to salvage something from a tragic situation (Figure 34).

The site is at the very north-western tip of the Range overlooking Dyserth, amid what was a very important area archaeologically from Mesolithic to medieval times and beyond. It occupies a narrow ridge, the successive ramparts totalling 3.5 km, mostly built of either turf-covered banks or dry-stone revetments. They now show as bands of rubble with occasional glimpses of what must have come before, with intervening ditches cut in places directly into the bedrock – a considerable feat. Pen y Corddyn and Craigadwy Wynt, south of Ruthin, are comparable hillforts on the Carboniferous Limestone.

To the east, towards the Flintshire Plateau, there are three or four ramparts where the slopes are less steep and where access is easier, but where the land falls precipitously away to the west and the Vale of Clwyd; a single stone wall was deemed sufficient. In fact the site is a good example of a contour fort. Overall, the rampart sequence is complicated and need not tax us here, suffice to say that there are two enclosures divided by an 'Inner Rampart', one of 7.5 ha to the east and a smaller 2.75 ha enclosure to the west. Additional banks and ditches in the enclosures complicate matters, but more than one period of construction is certain. There were six points of entry into the fort at least and four now remain. The excavation report talks of 'cleverly and similarly contrived entrances, each designed to lengthen, and thereby strengthen, the defended approach to the probable site of the gate itself, at the same time as producing reasonably graded approach tracks'.

There is much internal disturbance, the result of subsequent mining and quarrying, but the interior is generally sloping with sections of crags visible. Excavations revealed evidence of hut circles, largely confined to the northern half of the western enclosure with four-post huts in groups, but destruction of the northern half prior to detailed assessment clouded this interpretation. A zoning of different types of building could be similar, in part, to that found by Guilbert (1976) at Moel y Gaer, Rhosesmor.

The excavations from 1960 to 1967 in particular revealed many finds, though unfortunately their contexts were often not recorded. The collection included items of bronze, iron, antler, bone, stone, flint and chert. The worked antler and bone is of special interest and the finds could only be matched to those at Dinorben. The bronze items indicate that metalworking probably took place at the site; three are most noteworthy and of substantial importance: a bronze brooch or fibula of Early La Tène type (the first of its type in north Wales); a fragmentary iron cup-headed costume pin; and a fragmentary iron harness-mount in the shape of an openwork disc. Guilbert in the excavation report indicates that, by analogy, both the brooch and the harness-mount, and to a lesser extent the pin, are datable to around 400 BC. Radio-carbon dates from elsewhere date the site a little earlier.

These three artefacts give a fleeting glimpse of what life was like in the Iron Age Clwyds. The brooch, with a straight-profile bow-top, was made from a single piece of bronze 65 mm in overall length with spring coils and probably held an inlay of coral or similar decoration. Such 'Marzabotto' types are found as far away as Switzerland and have been dated to the fifth century BC. It would have adorned a cloak or cloth around the shoulders of the wearer. The bronze pin, probably used for a similar purpose, would have been of considerable length and was possibly decorated with tufa found locally at Prestatyn, a material used in Iron Age Britain as a substitute for imported Mediterranean coral. Smaller pins were probably for a person's hair or hat. This pin would have been very fine indeed and a much prized possession. One of the Iron Age's paradoxes is that the cultural sophistication of these people and their evident pride in and their appearance strongly contrasts with the crudity of their surroundings.

The horse harness-mount is shaped as an openwork iron disc and has counterparts of the same period (around 450 BC) from grave-goods of the Marne region. It could have been threaded onto the mouthpiece of a chariot-pony's snaffle-bit. As Guilbert says ... 'It should mean that we must see, even here in a Clwyd hillfort, men who drove paired draught ponies in the Continental manner, adorned with iron-forged versions of the Continent's La Tène I bronze caparisons'.

Caparisons (horses trappings) dated well before the end of the second millennium BC have been found in continental Europe, and a predominantly

Late Bronze Age hoard of harnesses was also found in the nineteenth century at the base of the promontory on which the Dinorben hillfort once stood. It was in the Iron Age, however, that the horse appears to have reached great importance, as the finds at Moel Hiraddug testify. In symbolism, the warrior Celtic mother-goddess Epona, identified by the horse, is associated with fertility and protection, and was a widespread deity in both Gaul and Britain (Green 1992, 204). Venerated and relied upon, the horse was admired for its speed, courage, fertility and intelligence (Green 1992, 210) and is a frequently used symbol in Celtic art.

Moel Hiraddug. however, also held other treasures. In 1872 miners under the direction of M. A. Gage of Rhuddlan were making a roadway on the eastern slope, near the top and outside of the innermost rampart. Buried under rubble and earth and heavily impregnated with iron ore, they made a remarkable discovery and one which has made the site one of the most important hillforts in Britain. Here, from the so-called 'tinker's hoard' were two much corroded sword fragments, several bronze plaques and ironwork from a shield.

Of great significance was the bright yellow bronze, formerly tin-plated, square plaque (now regrettably lost), possibly a decoration from a shield, box or chariot. It was about 15 cm square with nail holes to fix it in the four corners

FIGURE 35.
Facsimile of the triskele plaque from the Moel Hiraddug hillfort. Possibly decoration from a box or chariot.
NATIONAL MUSEUMS AND GALLERIES OF WALES

(Figure 35). The triskele (*trisgell*) pattern (in this case a broken-backed triskel) is a fine and significant example of Celtic art. According to Megaw and Megaw (1989, 232), it was probably of Welsh manufacture, since the copper ore from which it was made had a distinctive zinc enrichment and was proved to have come from the hillfort mines at Llanymynech Hill on the Montgomeryshire/ Shropshire border. These ores were also used in a Llyn Cerrig Bach horse bit and at the hillfort of Llwyn Bryn Dinas in the Tanat valley (Davies and Lynch 2000, 208 after Musson *et al.* 1992, 279).

The triskel, characterised by three swirling motifs from a central core, is an important design in Welsh Celtic art, and is recurrent throughout Europe. Discs and shield-boss from the Tal-y-Llyn hoard and a plaque from Llyn Cerrig Bach with bird-head terminals, together with another shield boss, all have this three-armed motif. The number three, embodied in the tripalism of representation of deities in threes (the *Deae Matres* of Cirencester, for example), or objects such as the triple vase from Chester, had powerful meaning in the Celtic world and this is supported by the Irish and Welsh literary sources where the triad is prominent (Green 1986, 209). This triple aspect of things may have been connected to birth-life-death, or seed-growth-harvest. Some four or five additional tinned three-cornered plaques, with concave sides and possibly an additional stud in the centre, were also found at Moel Hiraddug, but have also been lost. Whatever factor was assigned to the symbol, the number three was the common denominator.

Apart from the two sword fragments of just over 30 cm in length, the remaining object, and perhaps the most spectacular, was the sheath and crescent plate from the centre of a wooden shield – the 'Moel Hiraddug shield-boss' (Figure 36). The curved sheath covered the grip and the wooden central ribs, originally some 60 cm in length, and the crescent-shaped plates attached it to the shield itself. Strabo described a Celtic warrior with such a shield: 'their arms correspond in size with their physique; a long sword fastened on the right side and a long shield, and spears of like dimension'; in the *Tain*, a youth ceremonially comes of age by receiving a shield and spear from his lord. A shield was undoubtedly a prized object.

In the mid 1990s a model shield, with certain resemblance in decoration to the shield boss at Moel Hiraddug, was found near Barmouth and other model shields have been found in temple sites and votive contexts in southern England (Jope 2000, 250–51). Savory in the 1970s controversially suggested that the examples from Moel Hiraddug and Tal-y-Llyn might indicate a north Wales regional tradition of shield metalworking. The Barmouth discovery lends credence to his suggestion. The fashioning of miniature or model items such as tools, axes, shields and swords, although not confined to Celtic culture, was very much a feature of Iron Age ritual and religion and certainly appears to achieve a mystical status. Such small objects were probably for personal ornament. Again we have another instance of things not being as they seem; miniaturisation is probably allied to other aspects of Celtic symbolism, such as items being exaggerated in size, tripalism and the ritual bending or

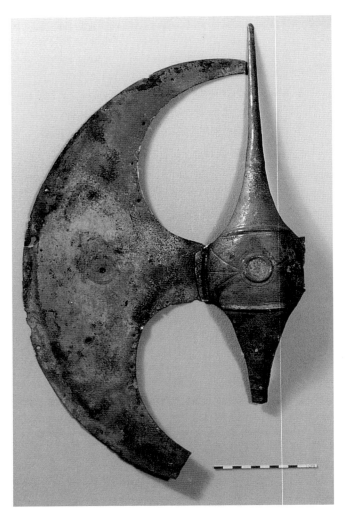

FIGURE 36.
The Moel Hiraddug shield-boss formerly adorned the centre of a painted wooden Iron Age shield.

THE POWYSLAND MUSEUM, POWYS COUNTY COUNCIL

breaking of objects. The act of making a faithful representation in miniature could sanctify the object as it could not actually be used: a 'conscious denial of utility' ... a deliberate removal from this world into that of the supernatural, as Green suggests (1986, 222). The finding of quantities of very small Celtic coins, called 'minims', in ritual contexts in southern England, may indeed also be acts of miniaturisation. The model shield from Barmouth, with its resemblance to the full size item from Moel Hiraddug, is no doubt a case in point.

At Moel Hiraddug, apart from a few flint implements, which could suggest Neolithic/Bronze Age activity on the site (a frequent occurrence on north Wales hillfort sites), no artefacts are earlier than 400 BC (Brassil *et al.* 1982, 82) and Carbon–14 dates calibrate to the sixth and fifth centuries BC. There was also no evidence of Romano-British activity apparent, in contrast to Moel Fenlli, Moel y Gaer, Llanbedr and Moel Arthur as well as Dinorben and Pen y Corddyn. It is now to Rome that we turn out attention.

CHAPTER 7

A Land Exploited: Imperial Rome

....

> From the point of view of imperial policy the Roman invasion of Britain was a predatory action. (A. L. F. Rivet 1958, 100)

Wales' extensive mineral wealth, especially its gold, copper, zinc, lead and iron ore proved very attractive to the Roman Empire. The metals found in the British Isles had been known about since the middle of the first millennium BC, and the voyages of the early Greek and Roman explorers no doubt had metals very much in mind. An additional attraction would have been slaves, to supply the economically dynamic areas of Gaul, the Mediterranean and, after the Conquest, southern Britain. Wales was, therefore, very much part of a British peripheral zone supplying the insatiable demands of the core to the south.

Pytheas of Massalia visited the British Isles some time before 320 BC (Cunliffe, 2001, 91) calling them the *Prettanik* islands, a name derived from the population name *Pritani*, or 'those who paint themselves' and by which the whole island became known (Ó hÓgáin 2002, 15). The two expeditionary ventures of Julius Caesar in 55 and 54 BC were really about prestige rather than conquest. Indeed Commios of the Atrebates, who had been sent to negotiate with the natives, turned against Caesar, later joining a rebellion in Gaul and carving out for himself a kingdom in southern England. These visits were only a prelude and in AD 43 the Emperor Claudius set in train what was to become a period of occupation lasting some 500 years. During this time the character of the landscape of southern Britain altered dramatically, in line with changing social structure and traditions.

Invasion and resistance

The Roman invasion force of some 40,000 men was commanded by Aulus Plautius, the first governor of Britain, and among its leaders was the future emperor Vespasian. Initially there was resistance in Kent under the sons of Cunobelinos: Caratacos (Caratacus) and Togodumnos, but the British suffered heavy losses as the River Medway was reached and Togodumnos was killed. With the arrival of Claudius himself with fresh troops and elephants, the great centre of the Catuvellauni, Colchester (*Camulodunum*) was quickly taken.

Some tribes sued for peace whilst others such as the Durotriges of the Dorset area resisted, with heavy fighting at their base of Maiden Castle. Generally, the tribal rulers allied themselves quickly to Rome and within five years the whole of the south was in Roman hands (Howell 2001, 39) and tribes such as the Dobunni of the Severn basin, the Belgic Atrebates of the south, the Trinovantes and powerful Iceni of East Anglia and the northern Brigantes all surrendered. When Publius Ostorius Scapula took command in AD 47 all of eastern and southern Britain was under Roman control and, after dealing with insurgencies among the Iceni, his attention turned to Wales.

Outside the zones of contact between the Romans and the British tribes, particularly in the south, the landscape of much of northern and south-western Britain, including Wales, would have remained more or less the same as it was before the conquest. That change in society did occur is certain, but that change would have been on a gradual basis as contact with Rome became more marked. It was not until the skirmishes of AD 47 between those allied to Rome and the tribes of the Welsh border, followed, as Tacitus tells us, by 13 campaigns into areas of Wales and the Marches up to AD 77, that any real contact was made with what the Romans considered the 'barbarians in the west'.

Six Welsh and border tribes are recorded by the Roman authors: the Silures and Demetae in the south; the Ordovices in the mid and north-west; and in the north-east, covering the area between the Rivers Conwy and Dee and including the Clwydian Range, the Deceangli (Decangi or Cenngi). To the south the Cornovii and Dobunni ruled the borderlands. It is also highly likely that other tribes existed, though they are not mentioned in any surviving written records.

That the *socii* (supporters or allies of Rome) among the indigenous people were of some importance to Roman hegemony is beyond doubt. Harassment from across the border into areas to the immediate east of the Welsh Marches resulted in continuing security concerns for the Romans in the Midlands and the West Country, and these could not be dealt with until Wales had been secured. No doubt gaining access to Wales's mineral wealth was also a motivation.

It was into Deceangli tribal territory that the first Roman incursion took place in AD 47, either possibly as reprisal for incursions to the east or to sever contact between Welsh tribes and the kingdom of Brigantia to the north. This was followed by a protracted and bloody war with the Silures and Ordovices to the south.

About the time of the fall of Camulodunum referred to above, Caratacos fled to Wales and subsequently built up a power base among the Silures in the south, the Ordovices in mid Wales and the Deceangli in the north-east, thereby becoming a powerful leader of the anti-Roman cause. From Tacitus onwards chroniclers have recounted the resistance of Caratacos against the Romans. Certainly he was a powerful thorn in the side of Roman rule and was probably supported by bands of free warriors drawn from supporting tribes such as the Deceangli, who were bound by clientage to serve in war and rewarded by gifts of some kind (after Arnold and Davies 2000, 3).

There has been much speculation as to the location of Caratacos's 'last stand' and whether it was in Ordovician or Cornovian territory or further to the east in Gloucestershire. Whatever the case, after a violent battle the tribal warriors, lacking the equipment of the Roman legionaries, were defeated and Caratacos's family was captured. He fled north to the Brigantes, whose Queen Cartimandua turned him over to the Romans. Taken to Rome, he and his family were paraded to the assembled throng in AD 50, but it is recorded that the demeanour of Caratacos so impressed the Emperor that he and his family were pardoned.

The resistance of the Silures in the south was also fierce and it was not until AD 62, after the demise of several governors, that Suetonius Paulinus appears to have got things under control. In AD 61 he took his forces through the territory of the Deceangli, causing many to flee to Mona (Anglesey), and attacked the island in that year. His infantry was ferried across the Menai Straits in special flat-bottomed boats, whilst the cavalry swam across with their horses. Tacitus explains the terrifying sight of the warriors that confronted them, between the ranks of which were: 'women in black attire like the Furies, with hair dishevelled, waving brands. All around, the Druids: lifting up their hands to heaven and pouring forth dreadful imprecations'. The Roman soldiers were initially struck rigid, but on the encouragement of their general they 'carried the standards forward, struck down all resistance, and wrapped the foe in the flames of his own brands' (Ross 1998, 68 after Kendrick 1928, 93).

Anglesey was renowned as the stronghold of the Druids and Paulinus subsequently ordered their 'sacred groves' to be destroyed. The campaign was cut short, however, by news of a fierce rebellion in East Anglia led by Boudicca of the Iceni. The savagery with which this insurrection was quashed came to the attention of Rome and Paulinus was recalled. After a subsequent period of containment, the years AD 69 to 98 saw a concerted effort at conquest and a swift operation by Agricola in AD 78, following the defeat of a cavalry squadron by the Ordovices, saw resistance in Wales effectively coming to an end.

Romanisation, industry and settlement

The extent of Roman influence in Wales can be gauged by the status afforded to the local tribes. The Silures and probably the Demetae in the south appear to have achieved *civitas* (city) status, with their centres respectively at Caerwent (*Venta Silurum*) and Carmarthen (*Moridunum*). The new regime sought to Romanise the tribal rulers and consequently to harness the land to generate rental or agricultural surpluses.

To the north things were a little different. The indigenous tribe of the Clwydian Range, the Deceangli, never achieved *civitas* status. They had no major urban or romanised settlements and probably came under military control; the Twentieth Legion was transferred to nearby Chester from the major urban centre of Wroxeter about AD 88 (Blockley 1991, 119). Alternatively the tribe could have become subordinate to the Cornovii, who occupied areas of the Cheshire and Shropshire Marches to the south and who held Wroxeter itself (Arnold and Davies 2000, 70).

In north Wales as a whole there is a lack of Roman military evidence, apart from a number of temporary (or marching) camps found in former Caernarfonshire, Merioneth, Montgomeryshire and Denbighshire. In Wales and the Marches there are only 29 such locations which could have provided bases from which the recalcitrant Welsh tribes could be subdued; Wroxeter is probably the most significant. No site has been located in the Clwydian Range nor indeed in north-east Wales as a whole, the nearest being a camp to the south at Penrhos near Corwen. However, it could be that there is a fort beneath the present Ruthin Castle (Burnham and Davies 1990, 3). Throughout these early campaigns the nature of the upland terrain was a hindrance to troop movement and to subjugating the population. Major rivers could have provided the main means of ferrying troops.

North-east Wales was very important to Rome for its metal resources, and became an important producer of lead in particular. Although the main production was centred to the east and north of the Clwydian Range, with works at Pentre Farm near Flint, Prestatyn and Ffrith near Wrexham and mines on Halkyn Mountain, sites have also been found within the Range itself. Silver was extracted, but was not of the quality of that mined in the Mendips, which contributed significantly to imperial coffers.

In the early years of Roman rule, the army was likely to have been in control of lead production, but after the AD 70s the Government took over and Flintshire pigs have been found bearing the imperial stamp. Later in the first century lessees probably worked the mines, but state control was eventually re-established in the Hadrianic period (Britnell 1990, 130). How the mines were worked can only be open to conjecture and it must be assumed that, as elsewhere in the Empire, slave or convict labour was used extensively here.

The complex at Pentre Farm, Flint, built in the AD 120s, was extensive and allowed the lead to be transported via the Dee to Chester. Excavations have found a high status building and fine pottery at Holt – the tile works of the Twentieth Legion beside the River Dee, and possibly used by a local official of some rank. At Ffrith there was a prosperous settlement, possibly associated with the legion.

At Melyd Avenue, Prestatyn there is direct evidence of metal production. The site had been a small farmstead in the late Iron Age around 100 BC but by the Flavian period Romano-British structures were in evidence. The nature of the site is uncertain, but it is possible that it was established by the Twentieth Legion to transport lead from nearby mines: a harbour probably existed to the west. By AD 90/100 there were two bronze smith's workshops with another in operation by about AD 120, one lasting until about AD 160. Copper-alloy goods were produced with fragments of moulds of trumpet brooches, dress fasteners, cheek-piece rings from a horse harness and chapes

FIGURE 37.
The small Roman bath-house at Melyd Avenue, Prestatyn, showing the remains of the hypercaust underfloor heating system.

(the metal caps of scabbards) being found, all manufactured in an essentially native fashion (Britnell 1990). A small bath-house has been excavated (Figure 37); tiles from the baths came from Holt. The settlement continued till about AD 160 as a metalworking site, after which it appears to have fallen into disuse when ore output declined, later to be reoccupied in the late third and early fourth centuries (Blockley 1991, 122).

Nearly a mile north of Dyserth church is one of the three entrances to Talargoch lead mine. This has produced Romano-British objects and is likely to have been mined in the Roman period. Davies (1949, 119–120) describes the finding of two bronze bracelets with snake-head terminals in a lead working at Meliden (part of the same mine) in 1704 and Pennant refers to an iron wedge in the fissures of Talargoch rock. In 1883 a Gordian III (238–44) coin was found in a washing floor of the same mine and between 1887 and 1899 others were picked up on the surface. Other Roman tools were said to have been found but, sadly, all now seem lost. This area of the Clwydian Range appears to have been a producer of lead in the Roman period and, if so, is likely to have fed the works at Prestatyn, from where it would have been transported by sea.

What we do have, however, is evidence of the continuance of a native north-east Wales metalworking tradition as suggested at Prestatyn. At Dinorben hillfort to the west, a pair of metal-workers' mould-stones have also been found in a post-hole dated to around the fourth century AD or later; the famous bull-headed bronze escutcheons date from about the late first century AD. The possibility of the manufacture of a distinctive enamelled type of brooch, of the type found at Prestatyn and Pentre Farm, cannot be discounted.

Apart from Prestatyn there is scant evidence to allow us to determine just how the local population benefited from the output of the mines in the area during the Roman era. The Prestatyn site had been abandoned by the early third century and Pentre Farm a little later in the mid third century. It is possible, however, that this decline marked the less secure times of declining Roman rule, but with continued taxation and even the working out of existing mines.

The Romanisation of the indigenous population, or at least its leaders, is exemplified best in southern and particularly downland Britain. Here large villas surrounded by extensive and fertile field systems have been found. In Wales there is no evidence for this sort of high living north of the Usk and Tywi valleys, the main concentration of such settlements being in the coastal south-east, particularly the area between Caerwent and Oystermouth associated with the Silures (Arnold and Davies 2000, 77), and a few further west in Carmarthenshire and south-east Pembrokeshire associated with the elite of the Demetae. None of these sites, however, achieved the scale or opulence of the examples in southern England.

This distribution speaks volumes. In areas such as north-east Wales and the Clwydian Range, despite local metal resources, things were that much poorer; wealth had simply not accumulated sufficiently to allow the construction of such ostentatious buildings. This possibly implies that agricultural output was insufficient to provide an adequate surplus and that rents just did not provide enough return on investment in what was essentially an unproductive upland environment. The Vale of Clwyd might be an exception to this, although nothing in terms of such a high status site has been found as yet, though there is plenty more work that could be done.

There is however increasing evidence of less ostentatious Romano-British settlement, on the flanks of the Vale of Clwyd, in the valleys of the upper Dee, Tanat and Alun, and on the coastal strip and the east Flintshire lowlands (Arnold and Davies 2000, 70). The valley of the Afon Chwiler can be added to this list. At Brynhyfryd near Ruthin, excavations indicate that some form of agricultural settlement, possibly starting as a military *vicus*, lasted till the fourth century. At Rhuddlan there is evidence of a similar site (Quinell and Blockley 1994). It appears that unenclosed settlement became the norm, particularly in the richer agricultural areas such as the Vale of Clwyd.

This distribution suggests that the Clwydian Range itself was essentially devoid of settlement in the Romano-British period, perhaps indicating that people mainly lived near good quality farmland and pasture. But this may not have been the case and we do have glimpses of a somewhat different situation. In sheltered areas, in locations such as Bodfari, for example, where there have been chance finds and a possible Roman cemetery, there could possibly have been a substantial Roman presence. The attraction of the mineral resources of the Alun valley may also have resulted in some form of settlement.

The occupation of Iron Age hillforts in the Romano-British period is suggested by archaeological evidence – at Dinorben and Pen y Corddyn, for instance, where a late Roman belt end-buckle has been found. Who left it, when and why is very much open to conjecture. The Dinorben evidence points to a chronology involving abandonment of some sites followed by re-occupation and a change of function during Romano-British times compared with prehistory. We cannot know for certain and indeed it is likely that things changed from site to site over time. There is no excavated evidence at Moel Hiraddug for use after the Roman conquest, for example, but Roman attack is proven at hillfort sites such as Maiden Castle in Dorset and Sutton Walls in Herefordshire. The loss to quarrying of the Dinorben site, where re-occupation began about AD 260 and lasted till the late fourth century AD, has not helped in our interpretation of the period in north Wales as a whole; nor has the partial destruction of Moel Hiraddug.

At Moel Fenlli and the pass of Bwlch Pen Barras below the hillfort there is similar evidence of Roman activity, although not of settlement. Two coin and ceramic hoards of fourth century AD date have been found here. The coins which came to light in 1816 and circa 1847, were of Constantius II (337–361) and Constantius I (306–337) respectively, the latter numbering 1,500. Nearby, during the excavations of the Bronze Age cairns at Cefn Goleu described in the last chapter, a probable hoard of 13 Roman silver and bronze coins of Vespasian (69–79) were found. At Dinorben eight coins of Magnentius (350–353) were found in 1921/22 but not in the hillfort context; more than six of Constantine I were found at Bodfari. At Dyserth, 21 coins of Valens (364–378) were discovered in 1860. Certainly the lead and silver mining area of Flintshire and Denbighshire was of considerable importance, as was the copper source at the Great Orme, Llandudno, until the time of Constantine at least (Boon 1968, 300). These hoards tell us that in the fourth century there was continued production in what were troubled times.

Ritual and burial

The Emperor Constantine decreed Christianity to be the favoured religion of the Empire in AD 312 and the former pagan gods were gradually replaced by one deity; by AD 337 pagan sacrifices were banned. Prior to this great change – and no doubt after it too – paganism continued to play a critical role in people's lives. A plethora of deities were venerated at both a wide and local level and superstition played an essential part in ritual. The local gods of former times, which were often specific to a particular area, river or spring, became Romanised. The most famous example of this in a British context is the native Celtic Sulis, goddess of the spring at Bath, who became equated with the Roman goddess Minerva.

Such cult-foci played a vital role in society, but evidence for their existence in Wales is sparse. Built temple structures are rare, although the second century Romano-Celtic temple at Carmarthen is a good example and the magnificent shrine to Nodens at Lydney Park overlooking the Severn Estuary has already been referred to. A native, non-Romanised, cult-site has also been suggested for a rectangular enclosure at Ruthin (Blockley 1991), but this is open to doubt (Arnold and Davies 2000, 130).

The existence of small objects capable of being held and kept on the person may also indicate a cult-foci and there are many examples nationally of small metal or clay figurines or models of animals and birds, possibly associated with native deities. In north-east Wales, the bronze figurine of a saddled horse, found in 1875 during the excavation of a grave at the parish church of St Mary's, Gwaenysgor, may indicate some form of ritual context. In north Wales more generally, however, perhaps the most famous example is the Llyn Awel votive deposit mentioned above.

Burials account for some 20 per cent of Romano-British cave finds; archaeo-logists see such use as ancillary to the occupation of open settlements within a reasonable distance of the site. Indeed it is thought possible to see both as contemporary. There is evidence in places of a continuity of rural settlement from the Iron Age and it is possible that cave use continued up to the third/fourth century AD (Branigan and Dearne 1992). Gilks (1989) lists fifty Late Neolithic and seven Bronze Age burial caves and rock shelters in northern

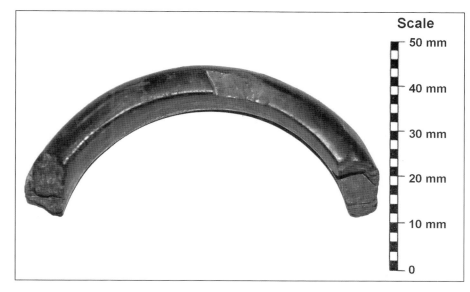

FIGURE 38B *and*
38C.
Shale bracelet
fragments from Lynx
Cave, Eryrys.
JOHN BLORE

England and as we have seen in earlier chapters, the limestone areas of the Clwydian Range were important cave burial sites.

Lynx Cave has already been outlined as having evidence of Late Palaeolithic and possible Bronze Age use and artefact evidence indicates that this continued into the Romano-British period. Blore (2002 23, 63–64) describes the finding of both a brooch of trumpet pattern and two shale armlet fragments in the cave. The cast bronze brooch is particularly fine, being gilded and exquisitely decorated with red and black enamel, silver and possible niello, a compound of silver, lead, copper and sulphur (Figure 38a). The head is 'late Celtic in style' and the brooch dates from before circa AD 150 (Branigan and Dearne 1992). Trumpet brooches of this type are thought to be of Welsh or Marches manufacture, though the Lynx Cave example is possibly not from the workshops at Prestatyn (Blore pers. comm. 2003). Two shale armlet or bracelet pieces were also found at Lynx Cave, the largest having an outer diameter of 94 mm and the smaller 80 mm. (Figure 38b). A Dorset provenance has been suggested. There does not appear to be any evidence that the artefacts were associated with any bone, but considering their fine nature it is possible that they were a sepulchral deposit.

A short distance from Lynx Cave at Big Covert Wood, also at Maeshafn, is the long-fissure Big Covert Cave (also called Maeshafn or Llanferres Cave) investigated by C. E. Hesketh and N. Pritchard in 1948–50 and J. G. Morris in 1954. Savory (1951) concluded it to be a burial site of Bronze Age, Iron Age and Roman date. At the end of an horizontal entrance passage, in the first 'entrance chamber' before the cave falls steeply away, Hesketh (1954–55, 141–48) made some important finds in a disturbed rubble deposit: a Romano-British bronze trumpet brooch attributed to the late first century AD, together with a small Bronze Age tanged and barbed flint arrowhead only 16mm long (Savory 1951, 175). The badly corroded trumpet brooch was larger than that found at Lynx Cave but not as fine. The passage continued and after some 46 m the cave opened out into a chamber before a rubble seal. Here embedded in the calcitic floor of the 'bone chamber', close to where water prevented further penetration, were the remains of five adults of both sexes, including the skull of an eighteen or nineteen year old, and the skull of a child. Ox tibia and sheep bone were also represented. Also found were two other brooches and a bronze ring.

The two brooches were particularly important. The first is possibly religious in function: a bronze plate brooch 3 cm long in the shape of a fish, enamelled on one face in blue and red. The second was 24 mm in diameter, with terminals moulded in the shape of ducks' heads, an unusual variant of a penannular type. Such a definite zoomorphic design is unusual; the terminals are usually coiled tightly back against the ring and only vaguely resemble an animal. A possible parallel example has been found at Lydney of a duck's head with popping eyes, but the beak is still pressed against the ring (Savory 1951, 175). The bronze body of the brooch had traces of possibly tin adhering to the terminals. A speculative date was given by Savory as the first century AD and the design was La Tène. The bronze ring was also of interest. It was two to three millimetres thick and 25 mm in diameter and coated with enamel; it could have been either a finger, toe or even a cloak ring.

These artefacts from Big Covert Cave, which regrettably cannot be traced, were clearly valuable and the deposit of such items in a burial context is the most likely explanation, although there is no direct evidence to prove this to be the case (Hesketh 1954–55). Again, as in the occurrence of bone in other Clwydian caves, a secondary deposition is indicated, either after excarnation or after part-deposition some time after death.

Orchid Cave nearby has already been outlined in Chapter 4 as having a Neolithic radio-carbon date. The finding of a decorated bone toggle of probable Romano-British manufacture (Brassil and Guilbert 1982, 5) suggests that the cave, in common with most of those in the Clwydian Range, was still in use many centuries later for habitation and/or burial.

Landscape and climate

In Britain taken as a whole there was a reduction in woodland cover in the Roman period. Indeed the greatest phase of Iron Age/Romano-British deforestation had been between 400 BC and AD 100 and this pattern intensified in the Romano-British period. In northern Britain there was a marked change to arable between AD 250 and AD 450. Some areas of Wales, as well as the Lake District, Yorkshire Dales, Pennines and southern Scotland all show clearance in the later Roman period and an increase in the size of upland settlements, as well as improvements in basic agricultural practices. During the third and fourth centuries plough technology improved and larger animals were introduced (Jones 1996, 205).

Most evidence in Wales at a detailed level comes from pollen investigations of upland sites, some the subject of iron-working and later abandonment. In parts of north Wales at least, woodland remained throughout the Roman period and it is suggested that some regeneration occurred where there had been substantial clearance in prehistory. This evidence comes from the north-west of Wales, at Llyn Cororion between Snowdonia and the Menai Straits (Watkins 1990), next to the ironworking site of Crawcwellt (Chambers and Lageard 1993), at Bryn y Castell in Snowdonia (Mighall and Chambers 1995, 1997) and at Moel y Gerddi further to the west (Kelly 1988; Chambers and Price 1988). South Wales seems to have been more open with cereal production (Dark 2000, 114–115).

By about AD 400, however, woodland clearance had largely ended with limited regeneration in some upland areas. No site has been recorded in the Clwydian Range and the state of the landscape can only be the subject of conjecture, but if the sequence is similar to the sites sampled in the north-west of Wales above, we can imagine a wooded picture throughout most of the Roman period, with regeneration of cleared areas.

The climatic deterioration after the Bronze Age resulted in increased rainfall and lower temperatures and a drop of some 2 degrees Celcius in the average annual temperature over the British Isles from southern Scotland southwards. A 1 degree Celcius reduction equates to about a two- to three-week reduction in the growing season. In upland areas such as the Clwydian Range these effects would have been sharply felt, the increased rainfall being a particular catalyst for landscape change. However, from about the last two centuries BC, and throughout the three hundred years or so from the conquest in AD 43 to about AD 410, there was a general improvement in conditions, with a warm, drier and less stormy climate. After about AD 400 things changed considerably, the climate becoming sharply colder and wetter (Jones 1996, 187–88).

Society and Roman rule

All societies can be cruel and pagan ones are no exception. The excesses of Rome are particularly well-documented, and as a result much can be deduced about the sort of life the various strata of society experienced in far-flung out-posts of the empire such as the Clwydian Range. Empire is about exploitation and undoubtedly life could be one of extremes. The details of how society was organised in the Clwydian Range during the Roman period is impossible to assess, however, as there is virtually nothing to go on. As we have seen, the Deceangli did not achieve *civitas* status and the area possibly came under military rule from Chester. It has often been assumed that, after initial skirmishes, the tribe was entirely suppliant to Rome – this may or may not have been the case. Rulers supportive to Rome were important and carved out 'kingdoms' as in southern England, or at least achieved the trappings of wealth. With the absence of villa sites to date there is no evidence for this in the area and it can only be assumed that the Clwyds were generally poor, despite their substantial mineral wealth, which was evidently the domain of Rome. No native coin was minted, as in all of Celtic Wales. We can glean a little, however, from the general situation elsewhere.

Britain came under the jurisdiction of the *Praetorian Prefect* of Gaul, com-manding not only Britain but Transalpine Gaul and Spain as well. The result of all of this was that Britain did not have direct access to the Emperor and bureaucracy increased, as did taxes.

The local administration of Britain was organised into four *coloniae* – *Camulodonum* (Colchester), *Glevum* (Gloucester), *Lindum* (Lincoln) and *Eburacum* (York), with at least one *municipium*, *Verulamium* (St Alban's). The *coloniae* were then subdivided into *civitates, vici, and pagi*. This may seem a stable system, but the need to meet the cost of the stationing of a large garri-son in Britain resulted in an ever increasing tax burden. This, coupled with military insecurity in Britain and abroad from the barbarian threat, general discontent, corruption and a deteriorating climate affecting agricultural pro-duction, put severe pressure on society as a whole. Both Strabo and Appian in the first century AD guessed correctly that Britain would not repay the cost of conquest. At its height in the second century AD the military garrison was about 45,000–53,000 strong, a tenth of the entire imperial strength. By the beginning of the fourth century, however, this had been reduced to between 20–25,000 and with a further reduction to as low as 12,000 later in the century (Jones 1996 161–66).

There are no records of the effect all this had on the poorest echelons of society, the *colone*, the peasants and slaves. Only evidence of the rich tends to be preserved, but it can be confidently predicted that the burden was disproportionate and that the poorer you were, the more you suffered. The rich were more able to evade taxation than the poor. The lot of those who lived in or near the Clwydian Range would have been hard, with exploitation increasing as conditions got harder. As Jones succinctly outlines (1996, 168), the result of this was that the poor actively sought patronage from the wealthy as a means of protection, the latter gaining a pliant workforce and a network of 'private loyalties' which corrupted tax collection and justice in the courts. Meanwhile freeholders were exploited by tax collectors and tenants by landlords' agents. This again forced more people to seek the protection of a patron, a process which led to the creation of a governing order independent of the state and a merry-go-round of corruption. There were also major changes to the rural economy as the fourth century progressed, notably from pasture to arable in the peripheral areas of north Wales, to feed the ever more voracious garrison in the face of declining climatic conditions and agricultural yields. At the same time the problem of expropriation continued.

The plight of the rural poor in Roman times was made worse by the sharp change in climate after about AD 410, with a colder and wetter regime causing widespread crop failure in marginal areas such as the Clwydian Range. Increases in arable in the uplands to meet the demands of maintaining the army would have taken precedence over the well-being of the local population. It is estimated that it took 53,000–61,000 acres of arable land to feed 50,000 Roman soldiers (Jones 1996, 205). The result of this unprecedented level of exploitation of all available land and soils in the more marginal areas was that the landscape became more vulnerable to the environmental changes being exacerbated by a deteriorating climate. Absentee landlords also increased in number nationally, resulting in less protection for the poor and a growth in imperial estates.

We can hypothesise that this sort of change occurred in the Clwydian Range, with more and more marginal land being used for arable to feed the nearby garrisons up until around AD 410 when the climate abruptly deteriorated. As yields decreased so the demand for greater taxes to feed the garrison increased in a downward spiral. Meanwhile from AD 406, events to the east took a turn for the worst with barbarian incursions into Roman territory. Unrest spread to Gaul and then Britain and this, together with economic and other factors such as the spread of malaria from the African continent, played a part in precipitating the collapse of the Empire.

CHAPTER 8

Invaders and Government:
The Medieval Period

....

> Wild warfare was carried on between the English and the Welsh,
> and when the latter suffered defeat, they fled to the mountains,
> wherefrom they showered darts and hurled huge rocks and
> boulders upon the enemy. (Marie Trevelyan, undated, 304)

When the fall of Rome finally came in the fifth century AD, it was not a sud-
den event. The processes which caused it had been operating systematically
since the late third century. How the retreat from Britain impacted on Wales
is difficult to gauge, but things would have been complicated by the threat
from Irish raiders along the coasts. Certainly the Roman garrison was substantially decreased and at Caerleon (*Isca*), for example, there was little activity
after 350 AD. The fort at Caersws appears to have been abandoned about the
same time (Arnold and Davies 2000, 143–44). By the beginning of the fifth
century the army was all but gone. However, some centres such as Wroxeter
managed to keep going for a while, possibly under the aegis of a local warlord
and it is possible that the elite took advantage of the legions' retreat to carve
out territories for themselves. Who did this, how and where is impossible to
assess.

Villas in the south also appear to have become disused after the middle of
the fourth century with possible changes in settlement pattern and movement
towards upland enclosures (Arnold and Davies 2000, 144). After about AD 326
no coin was minted in London and coin hoards of the fourth century within
the Clwydian Range on hillforts such as Moel Fenlli may indicate decline in
coin use.

A political system in retreat – especially one where the garrisoning of troops
is so dependent on local resources for maintaining control – is bound to
impact negatively on local economies. This in turn would have exacerbated
further the cycle of decline that had already occurred as a result of worsening
climate, increased taxation and deteriorating security.

Climatic change

Pollen evidence for the climate after the Romans left Wales comes mainly from upland sources. At the locations so far investigated marked vegetational changes are apparent, but there is great variability from site to site, probably indicating local land use change. At Bryn y Castell in Snowdonia, woodland cover increased from the mid third century to the mid sixth, probably as a direct result of the finishing of iron-working at the hillfort, whilst after that period woodland declined, possibly as a result of increased grazing pressure. Other sites show different patterns. There is no evidence of the pattern in the Clwydian Range and there is much work to be done here.

Over Britain as a whole there was a wetter and colder regime coinciding with what is generally termed the 'Dark Ages', but by the middle to late Anglo-Saxon period, from about AD 700, an increasingly dry and warmer climate lasted well into medieval times (Dark 2000, 171). In terms of agricultural conditions, it reached a possible optimum at around AD 1000.

Norse, Britons and Normans

To set the context for the Clwydian Range's medieval archaeology, we need first to canter rapidly through the wider events affecting the region. By the end of the sixth century Celtic traditions had all but disappeared from continental Europe but Celtic culture survived and thrived in the west, notably in Ireland, Scotland and Wales. After several hundred years of conflict Saxons controlled most of southern Britain, except parts of the Pennines, Cumbria, the south-west peninsula and Wales. Between AD 613 and 616 the Northumbrian king Aethelfrith of Bernicia attacked and defeated the Britons at Chester. The monks of Bangor Is-y Coed were slaughtered for praying for a British victory.

There are differences in interpretation whether the Britons of Wales and the north separated after this event or later (Stenton 1943, 78), but the country surrounding Chester was not added to Aethelfrith's kingdom and he was overthrown by Edwin of Deira before he could expand his domain. Edwin was a Christian and it was his aim to unite all Anglo-Saxons, but after taking the Isle of Man and savaging north Wales he besieged Cadwallon, the king of Gwynedd, at Priestholm off Anglesey. In alliance with Penda of Mercia, Cadwallon slew and defeated Edwin near Doncaster in AD 633, opening up Welsh contact with the north. The alliance did not last and Mercia continued as the pre-eminent Anglo-Saxon kingdom.

Offa became king of Mercia in 757. His authority was recognised throughout most of England and he soon turned his attention to Wales, fighting the Welsh between AD 760 and 784. Shortly after this he began the building of *Clawdd Offa* or Offa's Dyke between his Mercian kingdom and Wales. Offa's Dyke and its neighbours, Wat's and Whitford Dykes, of similar dates, lie only a short distance to the east of the Clwydian Range.

Norse raiders were less successful in Wales than England, and by the later ninth century Wales was also enjoying a respite from the predations of the Saxons. This did not last and fighting continued throughout the ninth century until Anarawd, son of Rhodri Mawr of Gwynedd, defeated the Mercian army at Cymryd at the mouth of the River Conwy. As a result, neither the Norse nor the Saxons could establish control of Wales for a long time afterwards.

Early in the tenth century the grandson of Rhodri Mawr, Hywel Dda, became king of Powys and accepted the overlordship of the English king, Edward the Elder, thereby increasing his territory. Edward's son and successor, Athelstan, gained the submission of the Welsh rulers at Hereford in AD 931. Although unpopular for this, Hywel later took the kingdom of Gwynedd becoming, in effect, king of all Wales, installing a more or less uniform social system (Ó hÓgáin 2002, 234). Tradition has it that he summoned Wales's first assembly at Y Tŷ Gwyn (Whitland) near Carmarthen at which each *cantref* (district) was represented by six men, and the laws codified.

When Hywel died in AD 950 fighting broke out among the rival dynasties, probably as a result of the continuing problem of partible inheritance. Norse raids increased around the coast, including that of north Wales. Fighting continued for nearly a century until Gruffudd ap Llywelyn defeated the Norse, English and his fellow Welsh between AD 1039 and AD 1055. In AD 1063 Wales was ravaged by two English armies and Gruffudd was subsequently caught and beheaded. By the eleventh century the danger of Norse invasions had subsided, only to return in the form of the Norse who had settled in northern France, the Normans.

The Dark Age period in Clwyd is well outlined by Nancy Edwards (1991, 129–41). A major problem is a lack of sound archaeological evidence, especially on the nature of settlement and society, with most information coming from later writings of the early church.

From what evidence we have, north-east Wales, unlike areas to the west, became an outpost of Anglo-Saxon influence rather than Welsh. Sandwiched between the powerful kingdom of Gwynedd to the west and Anglo-Saxon Mercia to the east, this was, as today, border country: *y Berfeddwlad*. Located between Gwynedd and the kingdom of Powys to the south, there was also a Powys influence in the area and it is possible that this kingdom extended north of Llangollen, as the Elise pillar indicates. It is also possible that the area became a source of conflict between Powys and the more powerful Gwynedd. Edwards (1991, 129) indicates that the whole of Flintshire and much of Denbighshire were included with entries for Cheshire in the Domesday Book of 1086, which together with place-names and recording methods, suggest a high degree of English and Norman control in border areas such as the Clwydian Range in the late eleventh century. Bodfari, however, was recorded in Domesday as a native settlement.

William I created strong earldoms all along the English-Welsh border, from Hereford in the south to Shrewsbury in the centre and Chester in the north, and gave them to trusted supporters. Spasmodic incursions began west of

FIGURE 39.
The ditches of Tomen y Rhodwydd, a Welsh motte and bailey castle of 1149.

Offa's Dyke and by the 1090s the Normans had built a series of castles to give footholds in Wales as far west as Anglesey in the north and Pembrokeshire in the south.

Unlike south Wales, there was no agreement between William I and the native rulers. By the time of William's death in 1087 much of north Wales, from Anglesey to the Dee, including the Clwydian Range, was under the control of two Norman lords: the Earl of Chester, Hugh of Avranches (from 1070) and cousin Robert of Rhuddlan, who had constructed a castle at Deganwy. The latter was subsequently killed, leaving Earl Hugh in sole charge (Ivinson 2001, 41). In the 1090s the Welsh rebelled, expelling Earl Hugh from north Wales, but still leaving most of the area east of an irregular line from Deganwy to west of Oswestry at the death of William II still in Norman hands (after Ivinson 2001, 43). These border areas remained in turmoil, with attacks, defences actions and counter attacks. Earl Hugh was killed in 1098 attempting to recover Anglesey, and the virtually independent power of the great border earldom of Chester came to an end.

From the eleventh to the thirteenth centuries Wales became divided into native principalities, of which the powerful Gwynedd in the north, Powys in mid Wales and Deheubarth in the south and west were the most important, with numerous lordships created by the Anglo-Normans. These later gradually assumed distinctive legal and constitutional identities as the 'Marches of Wales'. The lords of the March established their power by building castles, exacting tribute and hostages and encouraging settlement by English, French and Flemish migrants as farmers or burgesses in the newly created towns. Despite occasional royal incursion, expeditions into Wales were largely conducted by local barons. By the twelfth century Wales and Ireland had an aristocracy of Anglo-Norman descent with control over substantial territories and also a network of local rulers. Henry II demanded the allegiance of both, and claimed authority over the Welsh princes between 1154 and 1189. Eventually Gwynedd became the dominant power, as both Powys and Deheubarth became weakened by division and encroachment. During the twelfth century the Clwydian Range became part of the kingdom of Gwynedd Is-conwy (Gwynedd below the River Conwy).

Border wars and Norman control

Henry I ascended to the throne in 1100. The country west of the River Clwyd, including the Clwydian Range, had been freed from Norman rule by the turn of the century and there were no lordships through which he could exercise control. At first his attempts to woo the local rulers, which included trying to make Powys a client kingdom, met with little success. More forceful tactics worked and after moving against the powerful lord of Gwynedd, Gruffydd ap Cynan, through their territory, Henry forced the lords of Powys to submit. The situation in the north of Wales was stabilised for the rest of Henry's reign.

A period of peace ensued, but on Henry's death lordly Anglo-Norman and

Welsh rivalries came to the fore. During King Stephen's reign continual skirmishing between Powys, Deheubarth and Gwynedd altered the balance of power between the Welsh princes, and diverted attention away from fighting the Normans.

In 1154 Henry II came to the throne and stabilising the Welsh situation was to occupy him for many years. In 1157 he took a force from Chester to face the army of Owain Gwynedd, who had control across the Clwyds to the Cheshire border. They met at Basingwerk, to the east of the Range. Owain paid homage and withdrew to west of the River Clwyd once more. Peace did not last and after Henry's army became bogged down in the Berwyn Mountains in a campaign against a large Welsh alliance, he gave up trying to subdue Wales by force. After the death of Owain in 1170, Rhys was left as the sole native ruler in Wales. He came to terms with Henry, and with Gwynedd fragmented as a result of family infighting, stability more or less ensued for the rest of the reign.

King John came to the throne in 1199 and again the lands of north-east Wales figured prominently in the fight of King versus native lords. John initially gave his support to the lord of Gwynedd, Llywelyn ab Iorwerth, with a treaty in 1201. Although Llywelyn had married John's illegitimate daughter, Joan, relations broke down and John moved against him from Chester in 1211, only to fail through lack of supplies. Subsequently, helped by rival Welsh lords, John eventually succeeded and Llywelyn, seeking terms, lost all of his lands from the Conwy to the Dee. This left John undisputed master of Wales, but eventually the Welsh lords swept through the country and at John's death in 1217 it was Llywelyn who was left in control.

We can turn now to the most striking evidence of these medieval events in the Clwydian Range: the castles, which all date from before 1250.

The Norman castles

The Normans from the start made rapid progress in the control of the already anglicised north-east Wales, and their mounted knights, heavy infantry and archers, with their compliment of mercenaries mainly from Flanders, were virtually unstoppable (Ivinson 2001, 33), particularly in the coastal lowlands. Today, the main relics of Norman influence in the Clwyds and Marches are remnants of the motte and bailey castles which became the principal weapon in the control of Wales. An excavated example is Hen Domen ('old mound'), controlling the important crossing of the Severn near Montgomery, built by Roger de Montgomery, Earl of Shrewsbury, between 1071 and 1086.

The steep mound, or motte, the centrepiece of a castle, could be up to ten metres high, and was normally surrounded by a cut ditch. On top of the mound and itself surrounded by a palisade was generally a timber tower (although that at Chepstow was in stone), which functioned as a defensive stronghold, as a lookout and as a statement of power to the surrounding populace; like Iron Age hillforts, castles had a psychological function, and were a physical embodiment of subjugation. It was normal, but not essential, to have one or more baileys adjoining the motte; these were also surrounded by a timber palisade and a cut ditch, within which may have been additional structures for the garrison and servants' use. The Welsh did not make significant use of castles until the mid twelfth century (Pryce 2001, 84).

Hen Domen, used as a base for forays into Wales and subject to an extended excavation since the 1960s (Higham and Barker 2000) gives some idea of how a Marcher stronghold operated. A timber fighting platform followed the perimeter and inside there was an early chapel, a series of rectangular structures and lean-tos. Later, between 1175 and 1200, a three-bay apsidial chapel with possibly a timber bell-tower replaced the earlier building. A deep cess-pit, cut for latrines, could also have been used for housing prisoners. The motte, however, was the primary feature and was constructed by cutting a deep circular outer ditch and piling clay and turf from outside into the centre to form a concentric defence with a mound. Evidence suggests that conditions would have been extremely primitive (Smyth 2000, 94).

Designs were not uniform and much depended on individual surroundings and needs. Another Norman example, Twt Hill, built in 1073 by Robert of Rhuddlan, stands up-river of the Edwardian castle at Rhuddlan. The impressive motte with ditch stands 18 metres above the River Clwyd and is associated with a small bailey. In contrast the motte at Prestatyn, on marshy ground with a causewayed approach, is small at around a metre in height, though would have been higher when first built. Traces of masonry surrounding the bailey were noted in excavations in 1913 (Burnham 1995, 132). The castle was probably built by the Norman Robert de Banastre around 1164, but was destroyed by Owain Gwynedd in 1167.

Such fortifications do to an extent reflect the Normans' need for security in an alien land, but they were all that was needed to secure and control the landscape in the eleventh century. Fully kitted out they must have been an impressive sight with their high banks, deep ditches and heavy palisades. Mounting a successful attack would have been a formidable task (Steane 1985, 40).

The design was also used by the Welsh to effect in their internecine struggles. Tomen y Rhodwydd is situated near to the Nant y Garth Pass, which connects the Clwyd and Alun valleys in the south of the Clwydian Range to the Horseshoe Pass in the Dee valley; an important strategic route (Figure 39). The castle was built by Owain Gwynedd in 1149 whilst annexing part of Powys and retaken and burnt by Iorwerth Goch ap Maredudd of Powys. It was later restored with an added ditch during King John's campaign into Wales of 1212. This is an important site with the motte some 20 m across at the top and with a deep ditch below to the north and west. The bailey, some 40 m across with a surrounding ditch, joins the motte ditch to the south, which is causewayed at the northern corner. There is also an outer bank of ditch spoil on the south side (Burnham 1995, 139).

Toman y Faerdre at Llanarmon yn Iâl is also a refortification, rebuilt by King John in 1212 to repel Llywelyn ab Iorwerth (Figure 40). The rock-cut ditch was either dug or enlarged (Burnham 1995, 139). It has an impressive motte, some 6 m high by 25 m across, sitting on top of a rocky cliff above the River Alun, which it strategically controls. There is no obvious evidence for a bailey but traces of earthworks have been found on the north side near Plas Isaf (Jones 1991, 194). Its builder is uncertain, but Burnham suggests that it formed a local administrative centre. Unlike Toman y Rhodwydd, it was probably of Norman origin and could have been the caput of Hugh, Earl of Shrewsbury in the twelfth century.

These early wooden castles were prone to catching fire and this, together with improvements in the art of war, and notably in design of siege engines, necessitated stronger architecture. The stone castle gradually evolved with three key elements: the gateway, walls enclosing the bailey and the keep. By the thirteenth century, gateways were being strengthened by building gate-towers on either side and the timber palisade that enclosed the bailey became stone-built, with a walkway inside to allow observation and attack. Likewise, the critical structure of the stone castle, the rectangular or circular keep, became the norm.

FIGURE 40.
The Norman motte of
Tomen y Faerdre, re-
fortified by King John
in 1212.

There was only one stone castle within the Clwydian Range. Today there are only scant remains of Dyserth Castle, the earliest stone castle in north-east Wales. It was extensively quarried in 1914 and all that can be seen are traces of a ditch and vallum on the north side. The castle was constructed by Henry III in 1241, on the eastern edge of the Vale of Clwyd on top of a steep hill at a height of 100 m O.D.: the result of Dafydd ap Llywelyn Fawr's surrender of Tegeingl to the king. Finally destroyed by Llywelyn ap Gruffudd in 1263, the site commands the land towards the sea and the Vale of Clwyd, including the routeway between Holywell to the east and the Anglo-Saxon burgh of Rhuddlan to the west (Figure 58). The eastern side of the hill is joined by a narrow neck of inclined ground, making this side open to attack. It possibly had a strong but small masonry ward with a twin-towered gatehouse and two or more round or polygonal towers, each with stone outworks (Cathcart King 1991, 175).

The later Middle Ages

Henry III received homage from Llywelyn Fawr, though Henry did not consider Llywelyn to be the actual lord of Wales. This was to become a cause of great friction between the two. Three royal campaigns in 1223, 1228 and 1231 achieved nothing, although Montgomery was taken in 1223 and Chester annexed in 1227 and the area was eventually retaken by Llywelyn's grandson, Llywelyn ap Gruffudd in the 1260s. In 1267 Llywelyn gave fealty and homage to Henry near Montgomery, at which the Treaty of Montgomery legitimised the peace that had been agreed between the two sides. Here the title of 'Prince of Wales' was bestowed on Llywelyn, together with the 'Principality of Wales' (Pryce 2001, 80).

It was Henry's son Edward I (king from 1272 to 1307), however, who had the most significant effect on the social and administrative structures of Wales. The structure he implemented is evident in today's pattern of local government. The Principality of Wales, enshrined in the Treaty of Montgomery, neither had the strength nor the resources to stand up to Edward – in fact Llywelyn had seriously underestimated the financial cost of his treaty obligations. The wars of 1276 to 1277 and 1282 to 1283 ensued. By 1284 Edward had conquered Wales and both Llywelyn and his brother Dafydd, who had early on taken sides with Edward, were dead. At once he began reorganising the political structure of their principality of Gwynedd and a tour of Wales left lords and people in no doubt that he intended to impose his authority, with brutality if necessary.

The Statute of Rhuddlan of March 1284 was to be the blueprint for a legal and administrative system for Wales and created both new lordships for Edward's trusted followers and new counties. Three new counties were created in the north-west: Anglesey, Caernarfon and Merioneth under a *justiciar*, who exercised the king's rule on his behalf. In the east, the new county of Flint was bounded on the west by the crest of the Clwydian Range and attached for administrative reasons to the English county of Cheshire, coming under the control of another *justiciar* from Chester. Flintshire incorporated the cantref of Tegeingl or Englefield, the land of Hope, the land between Rhuddlan and Chester and Maelor Saesneg (English Maelor). Separate manorial or lordship grants had already separated this latter area from Welsh Maelor, which was eventually incorporated in a new county of Denbighshire, leaving Maelor Saesneg isolated. English law was imposed for criminal cases and the traditional Welsh structure left for civil cases. In 1301, the new dominion was given a new prince in the person of Edward's sixteen year old son, later to become Edward II.

This administrative structure for north Wales, together with the king's counties of Carmarthen and Cardigan in the south and west, formed the Principality of Wales, separate from the other lordships belonging to the king himself and to trusted nobles in the March of Wales. Thus the cantrefs of *y Berfeddwlad* outside of the new county of Flint were carved up: Rhos and Rhufoniog were conferred on the Earl of Lincoln, Henry de Lacy, making up the new Marcher Lordship of Denbigh, whilst Dyffryn Clwyd became the Lordship of Ruthin, granted to Reginald de Grey, who had helped Edward in his conquest of Wales. Rhufoniog and Dyffryn Clwyd were each subdivided into three commotes for administrative purposes.

These territorial and administrative gains were consolidated by means of the construction of great fortresses: Flint and Rhuddlan (which served as a base for campaigns against Llywelyn) in the north and Builth and Aberystwyth in the south and west from 1277; Caernarfon, Conwy, and Denbigh, the construction of which was delegated to Henry de Lacy, Earl of Lincoln); Harlech and Beaumaris, which was unfinished; and the refurbished Welsh castles of Criccieth and Dafydd's former Caergwrle (unfinished), at and after the end of the campaigns in 1282–83. The total cost of all of this was around £100,000 and, as a whole enterprise, Edward's Welsh wars cost him many times his annual income.

Edward's conquests also had a great impact on the environment of northeast Wales, not only in the exploitation of building stone, but also in the establishment of parks, forests and reserved woodland (Berry 1994, 7). These changes brought tension in their train and in the latter part of the thirteenth century the spasmodic insurrections of dispossessed Marcher lords came and went, but by the mid fourteenth century things had settled down to a degree. Wales was becoming a more cosmopolitan society (Griffiths 2001, 118).

Henry IV was a southern Marcher lord himself, but Owain Glyn Dŵr's rising of 1400–1410 proved to be a most serious threat to his control of Wales. Glyn Dŵr was a wealthy landowner himself from Glyndyfrdwy in Merioneth with grievances towards Lord Grey of Ruthin, whom he attacked first, followed by a series of towns in north-east Wales. Successes in the north and mid Wales were not matched in the south, and the involvement of others with grievances towards the Crown, and especially the Percys of Northumberland and Worcester, met a setback with Henry Hotspur's defeat by 'Prince Hal' –

the future Henry V – at the Battle of Shrewsbury in 1403. Land and towns were hotly contested and the outskirts of Chester were badly ravaged. Henry V's reign (1413–1422), however, showed a general recovery from the devastation wrought by Glyn Dŵr's revolt, accompanied by a growing distance between the lords of Wales and Welsh society generally (Griffiths 2001, 128–29). His son, Henry VI's attempts to administer law enforcement through the Marcher lords and lieutenants had little success, and accentuated these divisions.

The Wars of the Roses (1455–1485) were very much a Welsh dynastic affair. The triumph of Henry Tudor over Richard III in 1485 perhaps assisted the greater economic prosperity that was appearing in towns such as Chester, Oswestry and Shrewsbury from the mid-fifteenth century onwards. Drovers, clothiers and traders all depended on the sheep that came from the hills of places such as the Clwydian Range. In general Henry sought to pacify feeling in north-east Wales by assuring access to the law, and by repealing Henry IV's penal laws (Griffiths 2001, 139).

The Acts of Union of 1536, which superseded the Statute of Rhuddlan, created the kingdom of England and Wales, sharing virtually the same legal and administrative system. The independent ruling Marcher lordships were abolished and the two lordships of Denbigh and Ruthin, plus the lordships of Bromfield, Yale and Chirk became amalgamated, to form the county of Denbigh, whose boundaries, as those of Flintshire, lasted until the local government reorganisation of 1974.

The crest of the Clwydian Range marked the boundary between the cantref of Dyffryn Clwyd, later to become the medieval lordship of Ruthin, and the cantref of Tegeingl, and became the boundary between the counties of Denbighshire and Flintshire. Those who walk the high Clwydian Range today are walking along an historic boundary.

CHAPTER 9

Parishes and Pestilence: Church and Settlement in the Middle Ages

Of the 35 religious foundations in Wales before 1100, four surrounded the Clwydian Range, the nearest being at Llanelwy (St Asaph) with Llangollen, Bangor Is-coed and Abergele making up the others. The episcopal sees in Wales were fully developed under Norman influence by the eleventh and twelfth centuries, where before there had only been St David's. Four dioceses came into being: at Bangor and St Asaph in the north, St David's in the west and Llandaff in the south and east. During the reign of Edward I church and state came much closer together, with the king asserting the supremacy of Canterbury.

In the Middle Ages the church was the dominating influence on people's lives and permeated all aspects of belief. By the thirteenth century mass and confessions had become the norm. The church grew rich through vast endowments and the great monasteries, in Wales particularly those of the Cistercians, owned huge estates. Aberconwy's lands in north-west Wales, for example, extended to 15,379 hectares. The great abbey of Strata Florida in mid Wales had thirteen granges (largely consolidated independently-controlled estates) situated in five counties. Trade, particularly in wool, was the lifeblood of the monastery and rigorously controlled.

Valle Crucis owned granges in the south of the Clwydian Range, especially at Badhanlen and Creigiog. Possible building platforms and ridge and furrow with associated banks have been identified; for example at Moel Gelli and Moel y Waun. At high points in the Range these and flatter shelf-like areas possibly indicate stock management and tracks and green roads lead into these uplands, possibly to custodial areas. These features could be part of a grange landscape (Denbighshire County Council 1998). But all of this was achieved at considerable cost to the indigenous population, the Cistercian requirement for solitude – as at Valle Crucis itself – sometimes resulting in displacement of the local community.

The earliest evidence of Christianity in north-east Wales lies in the Latin inscribed stones dating to the fifth and sixth centuries AD. An example of these commemorations of the dead can be found in Whitford church; they initially came from Caerwys or Ysceifiog, commemorating 'the good wife of Nobilis' (Thomas 2003, 139). Many more examples occur in Gwynedd, perhaps indicative of Irish influence.

Very early ecclesiastical sites occur at Dyserth, Whitford and Rhuddlan where Edward I had intended to transfer the see from St Asaph. At Dyserth parish church there are the remains of a twelfth- or thirteenth-century AD Christian wheel-headed cross with cusped trefoils, possibly one of the last examples in Wales (Hubbard 1986, 343). It is recorded that there was another cross here (Owen 1886, 47) which disappeared in the mid nineteenth century. Such 'Celtic' crosses occur throughout Wales, and were erected to commemorate a person or event. Certainly, the cross at Dyserth can be compared with other later north Wales crosses of tenth or eleventh century origin. The most notable of these is Maen Achwyfan near Whitford, which is of Northumbrian design with Viking influence. It is one of the few remaining indications of Viking tradition in the area. Myth has it that the Dyserth cross originally marked the spot on the hillside where Einion, son of Ririd Flaidd, fell with an arrow wound whilst engaged in the siege of Dyserth castle, which once stood on the summit of the rock above the church. The Rev. Elias Owen (1886) in the *Old Stone Crosses of the Vale of Clwyd*, citing Pennant (1781), disputes this, indicating that it was the other and now disappeared cross that was 'Cross Einion'.

The beautiful setting of the church of St Michael at Trelawnyd, below the Gop Cairn and with distant views of Moel Hiraddug to the north-west, is the location for a very fine later churchyard cross dating from around the fourteenth century (Figure 41). The shaft is chamfered and the cusped panels on the head are of the Crucifixion and the Crucifixion with the Virgin Mary (Hubbard 1986, 446). The church itself, like most Clwydian Range churches, has been much altered and subjected to substantial Georgian and Victorian remodelling, but late medieval roof trusses belie its earlier origins.

The parish church

It was around the parish church that all village life revolved and there are many fine early churches in the Clwydian Range. Though we do not have space to focus on them all, we can at least point out some of the most impressive.

The church of St Mary, Cilcain is probably of the twelfth or thirteenth century, although the font could be early Norman (Figures 42, 43). The building is double-naved, having a western tower; towers were sometimes added after the addition of the second nave. Double-naves were a convenient way of enlarging a church and are a feature of the Range as well as the Vale of Clwyd and in this area they are exclusively of Perpendicular date (Perpendicular is a division of the English Gothic of between 1335 and *circa* 1530). The north nave at Cilcain (now the vestry) appears to be the earliest surviving structure dating to the twelfth or thirteenth century, but was later altered with Perpendicular windows in the fifteenth century. The south nave and tower also date from the fifteenth century, likewise subsequently added to and altered. Major restoration was carried out by Ambrose Poynter in 1845–46 and John Douglas in 1888–89. Other double-nave churches in the Clwyds are located at

FIGURE 41.
The *circa* fourteenth-century churchyard cross at St Michael, Trelawnyd.

Llangynhafal, Llanarmon yn Iâl and Llanasa; so to Caerwys and Rhuddlan in neighbouring areas.

The feature that makes St Mary's so special, however, is the magnificent Perpendicular south nave roof, with its alternating arched-brace and hammerbeam trusses. Angel terminals to the hammerbeams carry shields bearing emblems of the Passion (Figure 42). Tradition has it that the roof came from the refectory of Basingwerk Abbey on its dissolution in 1535, but there is no evidence to support this theory.

As is common in Wales, the churchyard is roughly circular, giving the Devil no place in which to hide. There are also examples at Gwaenysgor, Llanarmon yn Iâl and there was formerly one at Llangynhafal. There is also an interesting hearse house of 1810, adjoining the lych-gate. Owen (1886, 7–9) indicated that remnants of a fourteenth-century stone cross were sited on the south side of the church; today its octagonal stone pillar rests east of the chancel.

There are two doors blocked up on the outer walls – a priest doorway and another on the north wall. Blocked north doors are common in many old churches in Denbighshire and Flintshire. There is a vestige of superstition here in that, at the time of baptism, the door was opened when the priest entered to let out the Devil; this is the 'Devil's door'.

FIGURE 42.
The Perpendicular arched-brace and hammerbeam roof at St Mary's, Cilcain, possibly from Basingwerk Abbey.

FIGURE 43.
St Mary's church,
Cilcain in its village
setting.

St Mary's has other traditions. The north side of the church was burned down on Christmas Day 1532 on the occasion of *Plygain* ('return of light' or 'cock-crowing'). At this old Welsh custom a service of song began between five and six on Christmas Day morning and ended at day-break. Anyone who wanted to sing carols could, either singly or in chorus, after the reading of appropriate selections from the Prayer Book and with or without a brief admonitory address by the priest. The church authorities provided candles with holders made out of clay and home-made candles were also carried; the congregation was frequently the worse for drink. On that fateful day in 1532 things appear to have got a little out of hand. The north side stayed in ruins for 214 years until it was rebuilt around 1746 at the expense of Richard Davies, the Vicar of Ruabon. According to Pennant (1781), the cock was supposed to exert his power throughout the night during Christmastide. Records in the Churchwarden's accounts indicate:

1731	December ye 22.			
	Paid for 3 pounds candles to Plugin and carrage	–	2	0
1806–8	to candles for 2 Plygains	1	8	9½

(Simpson 1912, 13)

Later on Christmas Day another service was held, that of *Gosper canwyllau* (Candle Vespers) and, as at *Plygain*, the church was lit with candles at every conceivable point, with carols again sung. Today, of course, during the holy season such candle-lit services are commonly held in all sorts of churches, though they are perhaps not as boisterous as at St Mary's, Cilcain on Christmas Day, 1532.

Cilcain also has other traditions. The hermit, Eurgain, was the daughter of Maelgwyn Gwynedd, King of the Britons, who died of the yellow plague in AD 560. She was also the niece of Asaph, the second bishop to the see, who brought her up. During a period of religious persecution she retreated to the vale, 'under Moel Fammau', where she built a cell and lived a life of solitude and devotion. From this pious and exemplary life she got the name 'Eurgain' ('the fairness of gold') and shortly afterwards a church was erected near to the site of her hermitage and consecrated to her. The vale in which she lived was called 'Nant Cain' and the brook running from Moel Famau called 'Cain'. The hermitage was situated about three miles north of the present village of Cilcain. In his history of the Diocese of St Asaph, Willis states that 'Kilken' or 'Kilcain', was so called because of the brook Kain, 'which springs at Moel Famau, an high hil in this parish' (Simpson 1912, 6).

The church of St Mary Magdalene at Gwaenysgor is mentioned in the Domesday Book of 1086, which enumerated eight churches in the Saxon hundred of Aliscross. It is possible that a church existed on the site in Saxon times (Beer 1919, 3). However, the single-chamber church is very much the product of a possible fifteenth-century remodelling, with sixteenth- and seventeenth-century reconstruction and restorations of the 1840s and 1892.

The interior roof is medieval arch-braced with a Perpendicular east window. The font is early thirteenth century and, interestingly, a stone coffin lid was formerly inserted in the wall over the inner south door, later to be removed in Harold Hughes's restorations of 1931 and fixed to the north wall of the chancel. An early cross once existed on the site. St Mary's at Gwaenysgor, like the St Mary's at Cilcain, has a blocked north door (Figure 44).

As late as the nineteenth century, churches were not necessarily the pristine, clean buildings that we recognise today. The floor was frequently of earth and since a church interior was a place of interment, the earth could be mixed with the bones of the dead. The soil thus became imbued with religious significance; Owen (1991, 84) indicates that at Dolwyddelan in Caernarfonshire the soil from the church was used to prepare an ointment used to cure rashes and sores. At Gwaenysgor the earthen floor was covered with rushes as late as the first half of the nineteenth century, a practice often used in churches with no paving. Periodically, new rushes replaced the old, as at Eastertide. It appears that this custom ceased in 1839; at that time it cost three shillings to renew the rushes on each occasion. Easter was celebrated to a greater degree than it is today and the practice of Easter carols, sung both in church and house to house, was common throughout Wales. Elias Owen put an entry in the Churchwarden's Accounts at Gwaenysgor in 1808:

To for Ester Carol ...   1   0

The area in which St Mary's Gwaenysgor is located is rich in archaeological remains and Gop Cairn can be seen from the village. It is not

FIGURE 44.
Blocked north door at St Mary Magdalene, Gwaenysgor; a feature of the range.

FIGURE 45.
The late medieval
double-nave church of
St Garmon, Llanarmon
yn Iâl.

surprising, therefore, that the church itself has produced evidence of activity in the area in earlier centuries; the bronze figurine of the saddled horse, found in 1875, has been referred to earlier. A spindlewhorl of uncertain date was found under the floor of the church during the 1931 restorations and a Roman milestone was formerly inserted into the churchyard wall.

The church of St Garmon (St Germanus) at Llanarmon yn Iâl is certainly late medieval in origin. Some notable tombs and an arch-braced roof of that period remain (Hubbard 1986, 186), but there is much eighteenth-century work despite a John Douglas restoration of 1870. The churchyard is almost circular, as at Cilcain and Gwaenysgor, and is surrounded by roads (Figure 45). The shaft of a former churchyard cross is now part of a sundial.

The church is famous as a place of pilgrimage, and tradition has it that it was here that St Germanus solemnised the Easter Festival in a church formed of 'interwoven tree and flower branches of the forest' (Bede, Book I, Ch. 20 cited by Elias Owen 1886, 90). Thomas Pennant (1781) indicates that in Leland's day 'there was a great resort of pilgrims and large offerings at this place'.

Llanarmon is said to be the burial place of Beli, the son of Benlli the Giant (*Benlli Gawr*) who, legend has it, was lord of Iâl in the mid fifth century and from whom Moel Fenlli takes its name; the name of Bardsey Island (Ynys Enlli – Benlli's Island) may have a similar derivation. Pennant (1781) cites St Germanus paying Benlli the Giant a visit:

> but meeting with a most inhospitable reception, [he] was kindly entertained by a servant of the King in his humble cottage, who killed his only calf, dressed and placed it before the Saint and his companions. This goodness met with its reward; for lo! the next morning the identical calf was found alive, with its mother.

As is many places in Wales, a relict festival with pagan origins took place in Llanarmon on the day of the saint to which the church was dedicated. The *gwylmabsant* superseded former pagan celebrations held to venerate local deities and was one of the most important events in the community calendar. At Llanarmon the festival took place on 1 August and the subsequent wakes lasted a whole week. The festivities eventually died out in the early nineteenth century. The expectancy that this week generated can be imagined. No work was done in the parish during the festival and the local well-to-do gave

FIGURE 46A.
The fine fourteenth-century churchyard cross-head from the church of Corpus Christi, Tremeirchion, reputed to have miraculous powers.

FIGURE 46B.
Circa fifteenth-century stained glass in Corpus Christi, Tremeirchion.

presents to the poor. On the previous Saturday, a *Ffair y bol* (Belly Fair) was held, at which only food was sold.

> I did not sell it. I did not sell it. It was the churchwardens, and with the money they bought lamps for the church.

With this impassioned defence of the sale for £5 of the fourteenth-century churchyard cross-head to a 'Roman Catholic gentleman', the Rev. W. Hicks Owen, who became Vicar of the Church of Corpus Christi, Tremeirchion in 1829, walked 'rapidly away' from Elias Owen, who had asked him to explain the sale of this parish treasure. The cross (Figure 46a) was notable for its miraculous powers and was clearly venerated locally. Elias Owen considered it

FIGURE 47.
The late fourteenth-century tomb of Dafydd ap Hywel ap Madog (Dafydd Ddu Hiraddug) in Corpus Christi, Tremeirchion.

to be a 'Rood of Grace', more important than normal churchyard crosses, and it was celebrated by Gruffydd ap Ifan ap Llewelyn Vychan in an *owdwl* (poem) of *c.* 1500.

The church at Tremeirchion has fifteenth-century stained-glass fragments (Figure 46b) and some noteworthy tombs, that of Dafydd ap Hywel ap Madog (Daffyd Ddu Hiraddug) being a fine late fourteenth-century example with a canopy above an effigy of a priest (Figure 47). A late thirteenth-century effigy of a knight, possibly Sir Robert Pounderling, was found by Fenton in his tours of Wales to be 'covered with pews and trod under foot'. Indeed Dr Johnson when touring north Wales with Mrs Thrales in 1774 found the church in a sorry state.

In the Clwydian Range certain ancient rituals accompanied the dead. Bells, officiated by the sexton, were rung to announce a death, whilst the parish clerk preceded a funeral procession from house to churchyard with a handbell. The latter practice was recorded at Tremeirchion and Gwaenysgor and both practices were common throughout Wales. The bells were rung after a funeral at Llanasa and at Caerwys immediately after the grave was filled in (Owen 1991, 89). Funerals for the gentry could be very elaborate and Owen (1991, 86) recalls that when Sir Roger Mostyn was buried in 1642, the procession was led by 82 poor people dressed in white, one person for each year of Sir Roger's age.

Settlement

There is little archaeological evidence of settlement patterns in Wales in the early medieval period and there is none recorded in the Clwydian Range. What has been investigated tends to be higher status sites and the relationship between early medieval settlement and that of the Roman period. Indeed how settlement developed and was subsequently abandoned is unclear. As Arnold and Davies (2000, 159) point out, seven settlement locations dated from the fifth to the seventh centuries AD have been found in Wales, five in the south and two in the north (Dinas Emrys and Deganwy in Gwynedd). Their location appears to be influenced by several factors: the requirements of defence, access to the sea and the desire to exploit resources. Of eighth-century or later examples, five are recorded nationally, including Rhuddlan.

The coastal strip below and seaward of the Clwydian Range has been mentioned as being of importance in the prehistoric period and in Anglo-Saxon times. Rhuddlan was the location of the 'burgh of Cledemutha' (Quinell, Blockley and Berridge 1994, viii). This fortified site was founded by Edward the Elder, King Alfred's eldest son, after he succeeded to the Kingdom of Wessex. Rhuddlan, as a fortified town, no doubt, formed part of a strengthening of Edward's power-base in Wales, but could also be seen as a bulwark against Viking raids and settlement in the north-east, or indeed as a centre for trade (Arnold and Davies 2000, 197 after Edwards 1991, 139). Given the paucity of available information on the area, and indeed on Wales as a whole, it is difficult to make any assumptions as to the status, hierarchy or extent of

FIGURE 48.
Cwm village, below
Moel Hiraddug, has
clusters of Bronze Age
barrows nearby.

settlement in the Clwydian Range and we cannot say whether it was nucle-
ated or dispersed, bond or free.

By the late thirteenth century, however, when Edward I superimposed his
county structure of Flintshire, to the east of the crest of the Clwydian Range,
and the Marcher lordships of Denbigh and Ruthin to the west, there must
have been a well-established pattern of settlements and parishes in existence.
Churches existed by then at sites such as Bodfari, Llanarmon yn Iâl, Cilcain,
Gwaenysgor and Llanasa and people must have lived nearby to attend them.

In Britain as a whole, the complex landscape pattern of villages, hamlets,
farms and woodland, fields and waste came about as ethnic groupings from

within and outside the island interwove and interacted: in southern Britain Anglo-Saxon, Welsh and Scandinavian peoples all played a part. In north-east Wales and the Clwydian Range – a border region of continuing warfare between English and Welsh – there is little Scandinavian influence in evidence and it is the advance, retreat and intermingling of English and Welsh traditions that has moulded the spatial pattern of settlement, from the seventh century onwards. This theme of interaction is evident in the villages throughout the Range today. (Figures 43, 48, 49)

Dorothy Sylvester (1954, 11–12) outlines how Welsh society, communities and land were organised at a time when earlier tribal groupings were breaking down and becoming settled into lesser kindreds. By the thirteenth century, the *gwelyau*, made up of several kindreds, might compose a free township (*trefydd*). Here the houses (*tyddynod*) of the *uchelwyr* or free people were the units of a scattered settlement pattern based on pastoralism. This pattern was probably characteristic of the upland areas of the Clwydian Range. The townships formed part of a hierarchy; four *trefydd* made up a *maenol*, twelve *maenolydd* made up a *cymwd* or *commote* and two *cymydau* made up a *cantref*. The commote was, in practice, of greater importance than the cantref in political

FIGURE 49.
Llanasa village is
surrounded by large
estates.

organisation, as each had a lord with his own *llys* or court and a principal township (*maerdref*), with its own officers. In a 'free' township all land was 'equally partible' between all of the sons under the system of 'gavelkind' (the equal division of the intestate deceased's property) which resulted in some areas in a close pattern of small square or squarish fields. In a 'bond' or 'servile' township, on the other hand, the occupants were '*taeogion*' or servile tenants outside a kindred who held servile or unprivileged land, which on the death of the tenant went back to the township and not to the family. Dues and renders had naturally to be paid to the lords of the commote, the English Marcher lords, by both the free and the bond townships. Free men gave a rent of food (*gwestfa*), military service, death and marriage renders, and the servile tenants gave larger food renders and worked on the lord's castle and estates.

A large number of settlements in the Clwydian Range – with only slight variations – were 'townships' on the traditional Welsh pattern of small squarish fields and dispersed habitation. As Sylvester (1954, 13–14) outlines, at the time of the tithe survey of circa 1840, Cwm and Cilcain and Bodfari followed the typical pattern, but at Nannerch and Gwernaffield enclosures were not as complete. The process of small field formation was unfinished, and certain areas remained open, whilst others were enclosed. Ysceifiog, on the other hand, was more complete in its field formation. Tremeirchion was a large township, where a nucleus of small fields lay among larger open areas and, like Bodfari and Gwaenysgor, it had a small church hamlet as its central feature. This was also the case at Cilcain, although this township was much smaller in area. In the Vale of Clwyd, there were houses clustered around an open field composed of individually-owned or open common arable strips possibly associated with individual churches.

This social order of church and settlement, lord and tenant came under threat, however, from a factor outside anyone's control: the rat-borne 'Wrath of God' that came to be called 'The Black Death'.

Pestilence

Starting in Mongolia and the Gobi desert in the 1320s, the plague took some 25 years to reach Sicily, rampaging in the summer and autumn months, only to wane in the winter and reappear again in the following spring. From here it spread along the great seaborne and overland trade routes at a phenomenal speed, sweeping across France and the Low Countries, and in August 1348 it leapt the channel to 'land', it is thought, at Melcombe Regis in Dorset. It quickly spread to Bristol, Gloucester and Oxford and thence to London, and from that centre it spread over England and Wales and by 1350 had reached Scotland. In January 1349 the Bishop of Bath and Wells reported that 'the contagious pestilence of the present day, which is spreading far and wide, has left many parish churches without parson or priest ... since no priest can be found ... many people are dying without the sacrament of penance, adding that in such a case they make confession to each other or 'even to a woman' (Naphy and Spicer 2000, 39).

Black Death is the general term used for the initial outbreak of the pandemic in 1348, but further outbreaks of plague occurred in England throughout the next 300 years, until the 'Great Plague' of 1665. By 1361 there is evidence to suggest that the population was recovering but the return of the plague in that year resulted in another demographic decline of around 20 per cent, the second outbreak being perhaps half as virulent as the first. In the years 1369 to 1371 another outbreak is estimated to have killed 10 to 15 per cent of the population and by the late fifteenth century the plague was re-occurring every six to twelve years (Naphy and Spicer 2000, 41).

The plague hit Wales in 1349 and spread all over the country. It appears to have followed the great main trading routes to the west and north along the Severn from Bristol, along the Marches to Cheshire and north Wales. Griffiths (2001, 119–120) states that the lead-miners of Holywell were decimated and those who survived refused to work. Likewise, Rhuddlan and Denbigh were badly affected and in Ruthin 77 died in two weeks in June 1349. It is inconceivable that the whole of the Clwydian Range would not have been affected.

A peculiar feature of the plague was that it swept through rural villages as well as towns, although the second and subsequent outbreaks were more confined to urban areas. The impact on the landscape in general was therefore great; fields were left fallow and holdings abandoned, the skilled and able-bodied men died or left for the towns and there was a great loss of clergy. There was a general adoption of less labour-intensive forms of production, such shepherding as opposed to grain.

An example of the local effect of the plague comes from the township of Eryrys, part of the lordship of Bromfield and Yale which covered the present Wrexham area and north-west to Llanarmon yn Iâl. There is evidence that in June 1349 the plague spread from the neighbouring lead mining areas of Hopedale to Eryrys and neighbouring Minera, where it remained until mid-September. Lead mining virtually ceased in the lordship. The miners who survived refused to work in the mines and the population of the townships declined, exacerbating a movement back into farming where the market in land was already poor and where mining was undertaken as a matter of choice rather than necessity (Pratt 1976, 115).

The plagues re-occurred in Bromfield and Yale in 1362, 1369, 1379 and 1391, resulting in the loss of over one-third of the tenantry of the lordship. The loss of the lay brethren (*conversi*) was especially felt, and hastened the transition from the traditional grange economy operated by the Cistercians to a secular manorial land management regime. As elsewhere, the lordship was affected by an influx of disaffected people coming in to take advantage of the shortage of labour and the consequent high wages. The number of sitting tenants declined, and holdings were increasingly consolidated into small estates and farms (Pratt 1987, 7–17). These changes irrevocably altered the landscape and are still felt today.

CHAPTER 10

Belief, Agriculture and the Picturesque: The Post-Medieval Centuries

But the feeding of the rivers and the purifying of the winds, are the least of the services appointed to the hills. To fill the thirst of the human heart for the beauty of God's working – to startle its lethargy with the deep and pure agitation of astonishment – are their higher missions. (John Ruskin 1880, 78)

The Acts of Union between England and Wales of 1536–1543 were union only in name. In fact the Welsh were brought at a stroke under the English political and administrative system. The assimilation was so complete that by 1746 Parliament declared that whenever 'England' appeared in any legislation it should be taken to include Wales also (Jenkins 2001, 155). The arch perpetrator of this was Henry VIII's troubleshooter-in-chief, Thomas Cromwell, whose express intention was to bring under control all areas of the kingdom which enjoyed a measure of independence: Calais, Ireland, the Palatinate of Durham and Wales.

A land for the elite

FIGURE 50.
The secluded chapel of the Lady of Our Sorrows (Rock Chapel) on its wooded rocky prominence above St Beuno's.

With the growth of a centralised monarchy the power and number of the Marcher lordships was gradually chipped away by the Crown. Ruthin was purchased from the Greys in 1508. Between 1505 and 1508 Henry VII had granted the Denbighshire lordships charters of enfranchisement, thereby abolishing partible succession, emancipating bond tenants and allowing tenants to hold land by lease or copyhold. Tenants could also buy land and hold office and as a result many of Denbighshire's landed families began to emerge as the sixteenth century progressed (Evans 2001, 25–27). Nevertheless, the lordships were used as a source of manpower and revenue and still enjoyed virtual control of judicial matters, since there was no recourse to appeal from the lord's court. From the Crown's point of view, they were a thorn that had to be pulled once and for all.

As a result of the Acts of Union, the main centre of royal power, the Council in the Marches, was located at Ludlow. Monmouthshire was added to the Oxford circuit of the English assizes, so assigning that part of Wales to a 'no man's land', neither England nor Wales. The six north, mid and west Wales counties of Flintshire, Anglesey, Caernarfonshire, Merioneth, Carmarthenshire and Cardiganshire had been in existence since the Statute of Rhuddlan in 1284. To these were added seven others, created by dismembering the Marcher lordships at last: Denbighshire, Montgomeryshire, Breconshire, Radnorshire, Pembrokeshire, Glamorganshire and Monmouthshire. The shire map of Wales was finally complete, at least until 1974. The Clwydian Range divided between the counties of Denbighshire and Flintshire.

This wholesale replacement of Welshness dug deep into the structure of society, and affected those at the bottom of the pile in a disproportionate way. It was the Welsh gentry who fully co-operated and benefited most from the Acts of Union; they gained access to Parliament and London society. English replaced Welsh as the official language; primogeniture replaced partible succession for all of Wales; English law replaced Welsh (*Cyfraith Hywel*) and Parliamentary representation included the shires and boroughs. Until the Civil War, Wales was at least at peace.

At the beginning of the first Civil War of 1642 Wales supported Charles I for the most part; that is apart from the south-west and the north-east, including the Clwydian Range, where support for the Parliamentary cause was strong. Defections to Parliament and resistance to marauding troops were the order of the day in Wales, with the aristocracy more concerned with the protection of themselves than anything else. At the lower end of the scale the Welsh foot soldier suffered terribly in some of the bloodiest battles of the wars.

The execution of Charles I in 1649 heralded an intense period of mourning in Wales. County committees dismembered Royalist supporters' estates as the rigorous Puritan regime was implemented. The Restoration after 1660, restored wealth to many Denbighshire families but at the political level, apart from a few notable exceptions, the Welsh elite were tame and ineffective (Jenkins 2001, 158).

The increasing wealth of the elite during the sixteenth and seventeenth centuries was most displayed by the construction of fine houses, of which the Clwydian Range has notable examples. Both Brithdir Mawr (Figure 51) and Tŷ Isaf at Cilcain are fine examples of the hall house, where the principal room takes up the full height of the building. The former has a partition dated 1589, but Hubbard believed that it showed earlier medieval arrangements (Hubbard 1986, 338). Henblas, near the church at Llanasa, is dated to 1645 and full of finials, mullions and gables, whilst Golden Grove is a fine stone house with crow-step gables with finial decoration with dates of 1578 and 1604 inscribed (Figure 52). The setting is exceptional. However, the oldest house in the area was Hendr'r Ywydd Uchaf at Llangynhafal, now removed and reconstructed at St Fagans. It is of the late fifteenth century and a fine example of a five-bay cruck house, and retains its timber-framed outer walls (Hubbard 1986, 226).

FIGURE 51.
Brithdir Mawr, a notable sixteenth-century hall house at Cilcain, where the principal room took up the whole height of the building.

FIGURE 52.
Golden Grove, a fine
late sixteenth-/early
seventeenth-century
stone house with
historic garden in an
outstanding setting.

FIGURE 53.
Hooded tombs, as this
fine example at the
church of St Mael and
St Sulien at Cwm
shows, were symbols of
status.

In the late sixteenth century burial in a hooded tomb provided another way to display wealth and status. The earliest example in the Clwydian Range is for Sir Peter Mostyn at Llanasa, dated 1605; only the tomb-chest remains. There are two hooded table tombs in the Dyserth churchyard, one inscribed 1676, the hood having an angel on the underside. At Trelawnyd, a hooded table tomb dates from the early seventeenth century and has panel sides and a semi-circular hood. The most ornate and elaborate of all Welsh hooded tombs is that of Grace Williams beside the south wall of the church of St Mael and St Sulien at Cwm. Dated 1642, a base of open arched bays and fluted columns is below an open semicircular canopy with angel and skull and shields (Figure 53).

A clash of faiths

As a direct result of English dominance under Henry VIII, the very foundation of Welsh society, the Catholic faith, cameunder attack. By 1540, all of Wales's 47 monastic establishments, including Basingwerk Abbey to the east of the Range, had been destroyed without so much as a peep from the Welsh 'establishment', who were keen to get as much booty as they could. The populace was no better; at best not bothered and at worst antagonistic to the excess

FIGURE 54.
The well at Ffynnon Beuno has a large healing/baptism bath fed by water flowing from a pagan-like head.

and wealth of the monastic grange. The attack on shrines such as the well of St Winefride at Holywell, was another thing, however, and caused deep resentment. Throughout the Clwydian Range there are many local 'holy' wells; a stone-lined well named after St Germanus is located south of Llanarmon yn Iâl, whilst at Ffynnon Beuno a spring rises through a gargoyle in the shape of a human head into an enclosed sunken stone tank with steps leading down (Figure 54). This is possibly a healing or baptism bath. St Beuno, the seventh-century saint, may have preached locally (Jenner, undated).

Under the boy King Edward VI, a more radical strand of Protestantism was imposed on a reluctant populace. Medieval decorations to the walls of parish churches all over Wales were whitewashed or covered (Cwm and Llangynhafal churches are recorded as being once whitewashed). Only four churches in the former Clwyd county area have surviving medieval wall paintings (Edwards 1993, 11) and none exist in the Clwydian Range. Altars were replaced, screens and images destroyed and the English Book of Common Prayer introduced. As a result the subsequent accession of Mary in 1553 and the return of Catholicism was met with rejoicing. This did not last and when Mary's sister Elizabeth succeeded in 1558 the final phase the Anglicisation of the established church began. There was, however, still resistance, and holy wells such as St Winefride's at Holywell became rallying points for adherents to Catholicism. In an attempt to win over the people it was decreed by Act of Parliament in 1563 that the Bible and Book of Common Prayer be translated into Welsh: a substantial reform which returned the language to its rightful place. Gradually Catholicism became the religion of a foreign tongue, associated with the threat from Catholic nations such as Spain and Papal tyranny – as expressed in an unwelcome Papal bull of 1570. Establishment oppression and the translation of the Bible encouraged this shift in perceptions (Jenkins 2001, 162).

The rise of non-conformism

Puritanism was slow to come in Wales, spreading only spasmodically in an arc from the Welsh borders to Monmouthshire and south west to Pembrokeshire. The Civil Wars, however, gave impetus to a serious challenge to the Anglican order in the form of a host of Puritan sects, notable among which were the Baptists and Quakers. This did not go down well and the Restoration of 1660 was greeted joyously throughout Wales. The Act of Uniformity of 1662, followed by the Clarendon Code of penal statutes from 1661 to 1673, ushered in a period of intense oppression of 'Dissenters' and their non-conformist views. The Quakers suffered greatly and it was not until the Act of Tolerance of 1689 that things got a little better, although Dissenters remained barred from a wide variety of public duties and positions throughout the eighteenth century.

Methodism arrived in Wales in the 1730s and caught on rapidly, at first in the south and later in the north. Methodism was essentially for and by the people and initially appealed to the voiceless and powerless. Levels of literacy also increased with more books being available after 1695 when printing restrictions were lifted. It was more likely that children would be able to go to school, and the Welsh became one of the most literate and cultured nations in Europe. This was helped by scholars such as Edward Lhuyd (1660–1709), Keeper of the Ashmolean Museum at Oxford (1691–1709), who did so much for the understanding of Welsh history, environment and culture. With the establishment of the Calvinistic Methodist denomination, Wales became in effect a non-conformist nation.

In the Clwydian Range, as elsewhere in Wales, the rise of non-conformism resulted in the construction of that essential feature of Welsh hamlets, villages and towns: the chapel. The years 1816 to 1825 saw the peak of chapel build-ing, given impetus by the rise of the enclosed community as a result of rapid industrialisation and, in the Clwyds, the winning of lead and associated met-als. The chapels at Maeshafn, built in 1820 (and enlarged in 1843 and 1863) and the small vernacular Bethel chapel at Pen-y-fron near Rhydymwyn, dating from 1825 testify to this trend (Figure 55). During the nineteenth century

FIGURE 55.
The early nineteenth-century non-conformist chapel, now converted to a private house, at Maeshafn.

Methodism and industrialisation were the most important factors in the lives of Welsh people and to the latter we shall return in the next chapter.

The upland farm

Until the beginnings of the industrial revolution in the mid-eighteenth century, the mainstay of the economy of the Clwydian Range was agriculture and primarily the raising of sheep and cattle. As we have seen the clearance of woodland began in the Neolithic. By the eve of the industrial revolution most woodland was confined to the middle slopes of the valley sides – the result of further clearance to create new farmland. Stones were removed from fields, which were enclosed with earthen banks, stone walls and hedges. In the Range today, woodland clothes the lower spurs that thrust out into the Vale of Clwyd from the massif, as at Coed Ceunant below Moel Fenlli hillfort (Figure 56).

The farming system of the high Clwyds during the period to about 1800 would have been expressly linked to the lower ground. Here, meadows near rivers such as the Clwyd, Alun and Chwiler, were cut for hay and fertilised by cattle. A little further upslope the drier pastures with some arable provided winter pasture and feed. Above, the *ffrith* and moorland on the high flanks of the hills were used in summer. All of this would be linked into one seasonal system of 'transhumance', characterised by the lowland holding, the *hendre*, and the upland *hafod* and *lluest* smallholdings, which served as temporary upland pastures, to which traditionally cattle were moved on May Day (*Dydd Calan Mai*) and brought down early in November. Many families accompanied the animals and many earned extra cash by grazing other peoples' stock. As a result, grazings could become overgrazed with ensuing soil conservation problems.

This system began to break down from the sixteenth century onwards and by the turn of the eighteenth century had all but disappeared. The hafod either became used as a permanent home to meet the demands of a changing livestock economy from cattle to sheep, or fell into disrepair. From the sixteenth century, with the increasing demand for cloth, sheep gradually became more profitable to rear for their wool; they needed less daily attention than cattle and by the end of the eighteenth upland grazings were mostly devoted to sheep (Moore-Colyer 2001, 34). Flocks would have their own *cynefin*, whereby, through generations of breeding, each flock would be hefted, with its own upland territory. The animals were brought down for shearing in May and for lambing in the autumn. This system, although still operable in parts of Wales and England today (the Herdwick flocks of the Lake District for example), is itself breaking down as a result of intensive sheep production and, as in the high Clwydian Range and the Berwyn, modern enclosure of the commons.

In effect, two types of farm emerged in the Clwyds: the lower mixed hill farm, mainly concerned with the rearing of cattle as well as sheep, and the upland holdings mainly concerned with sheep production. The latter in particular were scattered and tended to be isolated from the community, with an

FIGURE 56. Woodland clothes the lower slopes of the spurs that jut out from the massif into the Vale of Clwyd, as here at Coed Ceunant.

average of some 12 to 24 ha; they were compact and self-sufficient. The enterprise was a family one, there being no surplus for hired labour and, despite the poor soils of the uplands, a small plot of land would be devoted to some cereals, basic food for the family and hay for stock. Added to this was the vital resource of the common, which provided summer grazings for cattle and sheep.

The lack of cattle in the hills today is one of the reasons for the spread of bracken, particularly in the *ffrith* and moorland margins of the Clwydian Range. With such a labour-intensive farming system bracken formerly played a significant part in the local agricultural economy and areas of the high Clwydians, with their deep brown podzolic soils, were ideal for its spread. It would have been used for bedding, as a source of potash and as thatch for buildings. Its use is indicated by a valuation of a farm recorded in 1866, which lies partly within the present Moel Famau Country Park, as having a 'quantity of bracken', presumably cut for litter (Brown and Wathern 1986, 374).

Flocks were usually Black Welsh Mountain and Black Faced Highland, both small and hardy breeds, and because of the 'free range' nature of the enterprise, Welsh wool tended to be of poorer quality. Flocks ranged greatly in size from 50 to 2,000 and, whilst the farmer sheared the flock, his wife would spin the wool into yarn. Most farms in the Clwyds had weaving sheds where the wool was turned into cloth before being sent to the fulling mill to be washed, thickened and dried. This wool production soon became the main source of income for the enterprise and was extremely important in north Wales from the 1550s onwards, with different areas producing different cloths. Oswestry market was an important centre for sale of this cloth as it was frequented by members of the Drapers' Guild of Shrewsbury, who bought it for finishing in London and Bristol and thence for export overseas and to America in particular (Clwyd County Council undated).

The commons

The commons are very much a part of the life of the Clwydian Range today, and cover large tracts of the central upland spine, particularly at Moel Famau and Moel y Parc. All land belongs to someone and in the medieval period it was vested in the lord of the manor. Lower echelons of society were allowed to use land belonging to the manor for daily essentials and in most manors there were areas of unenclosed 'waste' surrounding the cultivated areas, pasture and meadows of the settlement. 'Rights of common' had evolved from before the Norman Conquest on all parts of the manor to give an equitable share to all. The Parliamentary Acts of the eighteenth and nineteenth centuries enclosed these arable and pasture areas, resulting in the pattern of fields we inherit today. The fragmentation of land under gavelkind led to unworkable conditions and the Acts of Union finally dealt with the problem, leading to the enclosures of Tudor times. The unenclosed 'waste' of the less productive and often upland areas became the commons we know today.

The greatest amount of unenclosed land in Wales by the mid-seventeenth century lay in the uplands, but from the 1650s encroachment accelerated. Howell (1979, 1–2) details those encroaching and enclosing as coming from all strata of society. At the bottom were the squatters and, although some had to pay rent to the manor court, many enclosures went unchallenged. It was a Welsh custom that if you could build a house and have a fire burning in the hearth in one night (*tŷ un nos*) then you were entitled to the land within an axe-throw in every direction. Secondly there were landowners who were free-holders or customary tenants of the manors, who enclosed with or without the consent of neighbouring possessors of common rights or indeed the lord, sometimes with violent results. Thirdly there was enclosure by private landowners on the badly managed Crown lands and finally there were tenants, often encouraged by the individual lord. All of this piecemeal enclosure came to an end with the Enclosure Acts of 1801 which resulted in a marked reduction in the overall commons, although as late as 1800 some 25 per cent of Wales was still common and waste.

Common grazing was important to the survival of the upland farm, but with a rising population more land was needed to produce more output. The introduction of improved farming techniques, assisted by the new agricultural societies, such as that of East Denbighshire, set up in 1796 by the influential landowner Sir Watkin Williams Wynn of Wynnstay, Ruabon, encouraged the trend towards greater enclosure of the waste and commons. The gentry were obviously keen to improve the profitability of their tenancies.

Many small upland farmers suffered as a result; rents rose and grazings were lost. Those squatters who had encroached onto the common were soon evicted under the Enclosure Acts or suffered rent increases or even physical assault. Their fate was a disgrace. Enclosure increased during the Napoleonic Wars of 1793 to 1815, but after the boom of the war years depression ensued and demand for meat declined with much suffering in upland Wales.

The drovers

Cattle were important as well as sheep on the lower mixed holdings of the Clwydian Range and in north Wales generally. The Anglesey and Llŷn breeds were the ones most favoured in the nineteenth century (Moore-Colyer 2001, 26). Despite disadvantages in husbandry, the main advantage of cattle was that they could be easily driven and the driving of animals to the English markets became essential to the maintenance of the Welsh livestock economy. For the Clwydian Range farms the local fairs and markets at Ruthin and Denbigh were vitally important and it was from these centres that animals were driven to the Midlands, south-east England and London to be sold (Figure 57). The Range is criss-crossed by a network of local drove roads.

The history of droving goes back at least 500 or 600 years and probably much earlier. Strabo at the end of the first century BC described the kind of goods coming from Britain to Gaul as including: 'grain, cattle, gold, silver, iron, hides, slaves and hunting dogs'. Apart from grain, most of the

commodities in this list could have come from Wales, and it is likely that some did. It is possible that cattle were driven to England from the Clwydian Range in Roman times. Certainly during the fourteenth century the Welsh word *porthmon*, meaning drover, appeared in the literature, and Henry V ordered as many Welsh cattle as possible to be collected and taken to the Cinque ports to supply his French armies (Toulson and Forbes 1992, 9). By 1600 as many as 30,000 head were driven each year to England from Wales. Trade with the English Midlands expanding greatly after the Irish Cattle Act of 1666 (Moore-Colyer 2001, 30).

Most of the tales of the Welsh drovers come from the eighteenth and nineteenth centuries and are a matter of legend. Generally the professional drover was of good character, though tough and worldly. To ply his trade, he had to be licensed at the quarter sessions and be a householder over thirty years of age. Often the owner of the animals accompanied the drove, which may have been conducted by up to eight men. Sheep were also driven to England in flocks of up to 2,000 animals, as well as pigs. Because of the great difference in daily distance covered by each type of animal, they were driven separately; cattle, which might be shod, in a herd of 100 hundred to 400 animals, each drover accounting for some 100 animals. Cattle covered about 15 to 20 miles a day at a leisurely two miles per hour, pigs about six. By the mid-nineteenth century a drover could expect ten shillings a week plus expenses (Toulson and Forbes 1992, 16–17).

It was not in the drover's nor in the dealer's financial interest to have poor quality animals for sale at the English market and watering as well as grazing along the way was essential. Ponds constructed especially for the purpose were a feature of drovers' routes, as were inns. Often a Scots Pine or two advertised that drovers were welcome.

The picturesque and the sublime

Whilst the rigours of rural life were self-evident to those who had to endure them, to the cultured urban dweller a rural scene was all about the 'picturesque' and the 'sublime'. During the late eighteenth and into the nineteenth centuries ideas about landscape and its place in the scheme of things began to take shape. In his *A Tour through the whole Island of Great Britain* published in 1725, Daniel Defoe describes the Vale of Clwyd as: 'a most pleasant, fruitful, populous and delicious vale'. Vales were nice but mountains, for most of the eighteenth century, inspired in the beholder a feeling of awe-inspiring dread and were 'unhospitable' to the traveller. Gilpin wrote in 1772 of 'the mountains half-obscured by driving vapours; and mingling with the sky in awful obscurity'.

During the first part of the eighteenth century the countryside continued to be quite distinct and separate from the parks and gardens surrounding fine houses. From the mid-century, however, this was to change entirely and 'the park, simplified and expanded', was to merge visually with the countryside

FIGURE 57.
The Ruthin–Wrexham drover's road at Llanarmon yn Iâl, looking north-west towards Ruthin; essential to the agricultural economy of the area.

which, 'improved, was to merge visually with the park' (Fleming and Gore 1988, 88). Stephen Switzer in his *Ichonographica Rustica, or, the Nobleman, Gentleman, and Gardener's Recreation* published in 1718, has sections on woods, wilderness, groves and parks and advises: 'endeavour to follow and improve the Advantages of Nature, and not strain her beyond her due bounds ...'

The Reverend William Gilpin (1724–1804) was, with Richard Payne Knight and Uvedale Price, one of the three main theorists of the picturesque. He made nine tours throughout England, Scotland and Wales between 1768 and 1776, with the intention of publishing a series of books describing the rural beauties and antiquities seen, in imitation of the 'Grand Tour' to the ruins and mountains of the continent. Gilpin looked on the natural landscape in terms of the created landscape of William Kent or Capability Brown and did so with the eye of a painter.

Before the mid-eighteenth century Wales was regarded as a foreign land populated by strange people whose tongue was completely incomprehensible. Appreciation of the landscape of the country does have a long tradition, however, as the verse of Michael Drayton (1598–1622) probably referring to the Clwydian Range as seen from the Vale of Clwyd shows:

> When my active wings into the ayre I throwe,
> Those Hills whose hoarie heads seeme in the clouds to dwell ...

Most of all, the tours of the seventeenth and eighteenth centuries were undertaken by the worthy and curious for the purpose of antiquarian, scientific, religious or political enquiry. In 1773 and 1776 Thomas Pennant of Downing, just to the east of the Range, who also owned Ffynnon Beuno, made his famous tours of north Wales and totally changed perceptions of the country. A favourite author of Dr Johnson, he described the landscape in particular, but also brought to life the fauna and flora, cultural ways, architecture and natural resources of this strange but accessible land. In 1781 in his *Tours in Wales, Vol. II* he wrote of Moel Fenlli:

> Moel Fenlli ... is remarkable for having on it a strong British post, guarded as usual by dikes and fosses. This probably was possessed by a chieftain of that name [Benlli]; for Nennius speaks of such a regulus of the country of Yale; but as is too usual with our antient historians, blends so ridiculous a legend with the mention of him, as would destroy the belief of his existence, did not the hill remain a possible evidence.

He also wrote of the hillfort Moel y Gaer, Llanbedr:

> Beneath [Moel Fenlli] is another post, on a lesser hill, which juts into the vale of Clwyd, and is called by the common name of Moel y Gaer.

Above all it was the accessibility from England that contributed to the acceptance of Wales as a place to tour for pleasure and few upland areas of the country are as accessible from England as the Clwydian Range. In the late

1790s Wordsworth stayed with friends at Llangynhafal on the western edge of the Clwyds, describing that 'most delicious of all Vales, the Vale of Clwyd'. Later Sir Richard Colt Hoare, the antiquarian, was less enthusiastic from the viewpoint of the practical artist, being influenced by its wide vistas, although he did concede that the . . . 'mountainous boundaries to the east (the Clwydian Range) are well formed and finely broken'.

As late as the 1860s Wales and its landscape was still seen as wild, untamed and romantic. The title *Wild Wales* for George Borrow's book on his travels in 1854 from north to south is no accident. Here was indeed a 'wild' country teeming with the 'picturesque'; a place of hills such as the Clwydians and the lofty Dyserth Castle perched on its rock, the latter the subject of one of Henry Gastineau's (*c.* 1791–1876) coloured topographical engravings (Figure 58). All of this was within a stone's throw of Chester and becoming increasingly accessible by train as the nineteenth century progressed. The Chester and Holyhead Railway opened in 1848 and the linking Mold and Denbigh Junction Railway in 1869. George Borrow learned Welsh as a teenage clerk in a lawyer's office in Norwich and by the time of his tour he was fixated with Wales and its people and landscape. Surrounded by such wonders these new tourists put pen to paper and filled their journals with tales of the 'picturesque' and 'sublime'.

Nearly two centuries earlier, Edward Lhuyd was a friend of the Mostyns of Penbedw, Nannerch. His interest in antiquarian matters is indicated by this passage, which is quoted by Davies (1949, 269), between himself and Richard Mostyn and dated to February 28th 1693–4 (N.L.W. MS 2029B (Panton 63) No. i, p. 17 after Davies 1949, 269):

> There is one fair one [camp] above my house [Penbedw] that looks over the Vale of Clwyd, with a treble trench of one side, and a single one to the precipice. 'Tis call'd Moel Arthur. I suppose these were to secure cattle, etc. upon sudden inroads of enemies till the storm was over. The place below was possibly a place of action, where some French or Normans were concerned, for the Pass is call'd Bwlch y Frainc . . .

Still referring to the Clwyds he goes on:

> It lies only open to the Ocean, and to the clearing North-wind; being elsewhere guarded with high mountains which (towards the east especially) are like battlements or turrets; for by admirable contrivance of nature, the tops of these mountains seem to resemble the turrets of walls. Among them, the highest is called Moel Enlhi: at the top whereof I observ'd a military fence or rampire, and a very clear Spring.

Moel Enlhi refers of course to Moel Fenlli, which although not the highest part of the Range, can appear so from below. Certainly he was conscious of the 'military' effect imparted by the ramparts on the landscape, and the spring located on the summit.

In 1774 Dr Johnson, accompanied by his friend Mrs Thrales, visited Bach-y-Graig at Tremeirchion on his tour of north Wales. Mrs Thrale was a

Salusbury, a powerful and ancient family of the Vale of Clwyd, and Bach-y-Graig was passed down to her. The house was built for Sir Richard Clough and dated 1567 to 1569 and with Plas Clough, it is thought to be the earliest use of brick in Wales. Clough had been involved in the building of the Royal Exchange, contributing to its Flemish influence and supervision and Bach-y-Graig has a strong Dutch influence as a result (Figure 59). He also had trade in mind. As a partner of Thomas Gresham, he planned to trade from the property and link it by water with the River Clwyd. Here was a house essentially alien to the Elizabethan Welsh landscape, but by the time of Dr Johnson's visit it seems to have been in some state. Only two ranges now remain, much altered, and the 'six wonderful storeys' of the main block referred to by Pennant (in fact there was only one), were probably gone by 1817 (Hubbard 1986, 452).

Mrs Thrale's second husband was the Italian music teacher Gabriel Piozzi and between 1792 and 1795 they had built what was to be one of the finest houses on the very edge of the Clwydian Range: 'Brynbella' (Figure 60). The architect was C. Mead and the Neo-classical west front face with ashlar is particularly fine. The interiors have been attributed to Michelangelo Pergolesi, but Hubbard casts doubt on this. The gardens are informal with a landscaped park

and Mead was involved in their design but, apparently, his ideas for an ornamental canal were not accepted by Piozzi (Hubbard 1986, 451).

This was the era of the landscaped garden. Within the boundary of the Clwydian Range Area of Outstanding Natural Beauty itself are five examples recorded in the Cadw Register of Parks and Gardens in Wales (Cadw/ ICOMOS UK 1995). Penbedw, near Nannerch has a small nineteenth-century landscaped park developed from a late seventeenth- to early eighteenth-century plan to include an avenue of sweet chestnuts, oak, lime and beech, with wilderness and grotto. Also of interest are the formal and informal gardens with the remains of a canal and grotto, probably referred to by Edward Lluyd in a letter to Richard Mostyn of 1707: 'your artificial caves, which I take to be the only curiosity extant of the kind'. Golden Grove has the remains of a seventeenth-century walled garden, but it is the Edwardian terraced garden designed by Lady Aberconway that is of special note. The grounds of Colomendy at Loggerheads, beloved by the painter Richard Wilson, were considered 'picturesque' and 'romantic' in the late eighteenth century, but what we see today is essentially nineteenth-century. Talacre Abbey and St Beuno's have gardens of nineteenth-century design attached to former and present religious houses. Talacre has a fine eighteenth-century banqueting house set within a walled kitchen garden, possibly by Capability Brown.

Between 1804 and 1813 Richard Fenton toured Wales (Fisher 1917). Born in 1747, he travelled extensively in the Clwydian Range and visited both Corpus Christi, Tremeirchion and Bach-y-Graig. His visit to Moel y Parc, however, gives an indication of how visitors of the time viewed the Clwydian landscape and its antiquarian past:

> In our way down to Maes Mynnan rode over the edge of a beautiful
> wooded dingle belonging to Sir Thomas Mostyn. It seems Maes Mynnan
> was occasionally the residence of the last Llewelyn and his Palace, if
> Palace it might be called, was said to have stood under the Hill exactly
> opposite to the present House, just on the Margin of the little stream,
> and that he had a large inclosure behind occupying a great tract of the
> Hills for his Venison, called to this day Moel y Park, and traces of the
> Fence that enclosed it may be seen somewhere under this Hill. There was
> dug up some years back an earthen Vessel with some trinkets, and one
> gold chain was sold at Chester for £140.

The 'earthen Vessel with some trinkets' refers to the Coed Bedw hoard outlined in Chapter 5.

This obsession with the picturesque and romantic, with applied dramatic overtones which never existed in real life, had to be enhanced in the psyche by the addition of man-made accoutrements. No self-respecting gentleman would be without his folly. Grottoes (the origin of the word 'grotesque'), monuments, artificial lakes, watercourses and 'natural' scenes contrived by extensive construction and landscaping, were the order of the day. Elements of the foreign and antiquarian were often embodied in the design, with Greek,

Roman, Turkish and Egyptian references being especially popular. The Doric stone doorcase at Brynbella is such a device. Nowhere was the dramatic so much in evidence though than at Moel Famau. Between 1810 and 1812, at its summit at 554 m O.D., a great tower was erected to commemorate the Golden Jubilee of the 72-year-old George III. Here indeed was a statement of the age.

Some £6,000 was raised by public subscription, with money also forthcoming from the local aristocracy and the Prince Regent. The architect was Thomas Harrison of Chester and his proposal was for an obelisk some 49 m in height, to be the first Egyptian-style monument to be built in Britain. The foundation stone was laid by Lord Kenyon on 25 October 1810, but soon the enterprise ran into funding problems. To transport vast and heavy quantities of material to such a peak, renowned for unpredictable weather at the best of times, took its toll and the tower was modified by Harrison during building. This resulted in three diminishing tiers, the top one being the obelisk itself and the bottom a massive stone base with a blank doorway on each of its faces and square bastions.

On 1 November 1862 a ferocious storm blew down the upper stages of the tower and despite a number of proposals to re-build it to its former glory, it remained derelict with its top tiers cleared for safety reasons; only the massive bottom stage remaining. A project undertaken in 1970, to commemorate the investiture of the Prince of Wales a year earlier, involved the construction out of the ruins of a viewing platform and diorama (Figure 61). The tower is still a popular destination for the many thousands who climb Moel Famau each year.

Black's Picturesque Guide to Wales of 1874, designed to 'render assistance to those who may be desirous of exploring this country, or of visiting any portion of it' was expressly published for that much maligned creature, 'the tourist'. Here were exhortations to climb 'Moel Fammau' where: 'the prospect will amply repay the trifling exertion demanded by the easy ascent'. The book gave details of what to see along the line of the Chester to Holyhead Railway which then formed part of the London and North Western system. Tourism had very definitely arrived.

Gerard Manley Hopkins and St Beuno's

St Beuno's College is a Jesuit foundation. The original buildings of 1846–1849 were by the Victorian architect Joseph Aloysius Hansom (1802–82) and formed the first of a succession of Pugin-inspired collegiate buildings of the mid-nineteenth century which achieved their zenith with Butterfield's Keble College, Oxford, a building much deplored by Ruskin. It occupies a magnificent position on the slopes of the Clwydian Range near Tremeirchion, overlooking the Vale of Clwyd with a view to the sea. The south front climbing the hill is very impressive, with tower and oriel to the west main building, and there are additions of a north entrance court by Hansom & Co. of 1873–74 (Figure 62). The chapel, part of Hansom's original work, has a

St. Beuno's College, St. Asaph

Valentines Series

FIGURE 61.
The Jubilee Tower,
Moel Famau as it is
today.

FIGURE 62.
St Beuno's College,
c.1915 where Gerard
Manley Hopkins
studied for the
priesthood between
1874 and 1877.

FLINTSHIRE COUNTY
COUNCIL

rib-vaulted polygonal apse and hammerbeam roof with angels. The chapel of the Lady of Our Sorrows (Rock Chapel), perched on a rocky outcrop above the college is like some miniature folly of the eighteenth century (Figure 50). Built in 1866 to a design of Father Innatius Scoles, a student at the time, it has a tower with slender spire and a semi-circular apse.

It was at St Beuno's that Gerard Manley Hopkins (1844–1889), the Jesuit priest and poet, came to study theology in 1874 in preparation for the priesthood. He was ordained in 1877 in the college chapel. He found inspiration here and was captivated by the sheer beauty of the place and surrounding landscape, and became enthralled by the Welsh language and people. One third of his mature poetry was written whilst at the college (Thomas 1971–72, 98). Just after he arrived he wrote to his father:

> The house stands on a steep hillside, it commands the long-drawn valley of the Clwyd to the sea, a vast prospect, and opposite is Snowdon and its range, just now it being bright visible but coming and going with the weather. The air seems to me very fresh and wholesome. [The house] is built of limestone, decent outside, skimpin within, Gothic, like Lancing

FIGURE 63.
Ruined farm above Plas Dolben, Llangynhafal. Such remains are features of the high Clwyds.

College done worse. The staircases, galleries, and bopeeps are inexpressible: it takes a fortnight to learn them ... The garden is all heights, terraces, Excelsiors, misty mountain tops, seats up trees called Crow's Nests, flight of steps seemingly up to heaven lined with burning aspiration of scarlet geraniums.

The landscape of Wales and the Clwydian Range and Vale of Clwyd in particular, gave Hopkin's inspiration. He saw the beauty of the natural landscape, not from the detached viewpoint of the picturesque school, but as an embodiment of the munificence of the Creator. This was embodied in his sonnet 'Pied Beauty' of 1877, written at St Beuno's:

> Glory be to God for dappled things-
> For skies of couple-colour as a brinded cow;
> For rose-moles all in stipple upon trout that swim;
> Fresh-firecoal chestnut falls; finches' wings;
> Landscape plotted and pieced-fold, fallow, and plough;
> And all trades, their gear and tackle and trim.

Hopkins' stay in the Clwydian Range certainly fostered this outpouring of creativity and he and his companions explored the area widely. He managed to capture the change of temperament in the landscape perfectly; on one occasion *melancholy*:

> The cleave in which Bodfari and Caerwys lies was close below. It was a leaden sky, braided or roped with cloud, and the earth in dead colours, grave but distinct' ...
> ... on another *glad*:
> Clarke and I made one of the only two couples that reached Moel Fammau. When we had come down into the valley the day became very beautiful. Looking up along a white churchtower I caught a lively sight – a flock of seagulls wheeling and sailing high up in the air, sparkles of white as bright as snowballs in the vivid blue.

His stay is personified by one of his most famous verses; from 'Moonrise' of 1876:

> I awoke in the Midsummer not-to-call night, in the white and the walk
>   of the morning:
> The moon, dwindled and thinned to the fringe of a fingernail held to the
>   candle,
> Or paring of paradisaical fruit, lovely in waning but lustreless,
> Stepped from the stool, drew back from the barrow, of dark Maenefa
>   the mountain ...

'Dark Maenefa' was Moel Maenefa, situated behind the college.

A dire poverty within

By the 1850s John Ruskin (1819–1900), surely one of the truly great Victorians, had become acutely aware of the social and moral implications of the picturesque and of the desperate poverty that was suffered by those who lived in the:

> rugged highland cottage ... but as I looked to-day at the unhealthy face and melancholy, apathetic mien of the man in the boat, pushing his load of peats along the ditch, and of the people, men and women, who sat spinning gloomily in the picturesque cottages, I could not help feeling how many suffering persons must pay for my picturesque subject, and my happy walk (Diaries, II, 493 quoted by Landlow 2003, 5).

People in the landscape, in effect, were not to be seen as purely objects in a picturesque scene, but as an integral and living part of it. Ruskin's is so different from Wordsworth's view of nature. It is easy to concentrate on the large and the fine, but Ruskin was clearly uneasy about the lot of his less fortunate fellow men who contributed so much to the embodiment of the 'picturesque' beloved by eighteenth- and nineteenth-century society.

Examples of the remains of these 'picturesque' vernacular dwellings still exist in the Clwydian Range, but now as outer walls and piles of stone (Figure 63, page 143). Romantic the rugged cottage may have seemed, but comfortable it was certainly not and the picturesque frequently masked a dire poverty within.

CHAPTER 11

Mines, Engine Houses and Tracks: Water, Water, Everywhere

....

In a morning stroll along the banks of the Alun, a beautiful little
stream which flows down the Welsh hills and throws itself into
the River Dee ...
(Washington Irving, 1783–1859, quoted in Roberts 1992)

Industry developed very differently in the east and western parts of the
Clwydian Range and although it is large-scale quarrying that now dominates
the scene, vestiges of the past are very much part of the present day landscape.

Small-scale enterprises in the west

In the western half of the Clwydian Range small-scale enterprises once dominated, particularly in the activities of agricultural processing, metalwork such as
smithing, quarrying and mineral working. The smith was a necessary part of
the local community and was relied upon, to literally 'keep the wheels turn-
ing'. Throughout the area, in the medieval and post-medieval periods, the
local wayside quarry would have been essential for the maintenance of trackways and the construction of houses and walls, and examples abound
throughout the Range, as on the shaly slopes of Moel Arthur.

Minerals were also spasmodically investigated and worked in the west.
There were a number of small-scale gold, lead and barytes mining enterprises
of the 1890s on Moel Dywyll near Moel Famau and a small nineteenth century gold mine and trials on the western slopes of Moel Arthur nearby.
Simpson (1912, 7) describes gold mining taking place at Cilcain:

... but the results did not justify its continuance as the yield was not
sufficient to pay a profit on the working – though some assert that gold
may probably be found in valuable quantities near.

Lead also appears to have been investigated near Llangwyfan at the edge of
the Vale of Clwyd.

The largest mineral enterprise in the west, however, was a haematite mine
at Coed Llan to the north of the village of Bodfari, worked between 1877 and

FIGURE 64.
The Pennant Engine
House served a lead,
silver and barytes mine.

1909. All that can be seen today are remains of the agent's house and workshop, the mine shaft and a possible horse whim. Quarrying (Coed-y-llan quarry) and mining ceased in the twentieth century, but the remains of the Partington Steel and Iron Company's railway quarry sidings, from construction of the Mold and Denbigh Junction Railway in 1924, are still visible. It was in the area of the eastern Clwyds, however, that industry developed on a much larger scale from the seventeenth century onwards.

Mining in the east

North-east Wales became an important producer of lead and zinc in Roman times, as outlined in Chapter 7, continuing throughout the medieval period, but it was not until the late seventeenth and eighteenth centuries that

FIGURE 65.
The River Alun flows underground in dry periods, showing its rocky bed.

significant expansion took place (Grenter and Williams 1991, 224). By the last half of the nineteenth century the area produced over 10 per cent of all the lead ore mined in Britain and nearly 30 per cent of zinc. This expansion was particularly significant in the Clwydian Range, and was centred on the limestone of the Alun valley.

The River Alun is a typical limestone river flowing through a 'karst' landscape of steep gorges and swallow holes. Downstream of Loggerheads the river disappears into its bed in dry periods during the summer to flow underground and re-appear further downstream (Figure 65). Edward Lhuyd noticed this phenomenon in the late seventeenth century. This purely natural action of the river caused severe problems for the lead mines that sprang up along its course from Loggerheads downstream to Rhydymwyn from the mid seventeenth century onwards, to exploit the succession of east to west running mineral veins. At Rhydymwyn the river flows out of the Clwydian Range to take a southerly course to Mold and thence to the Dee.

The ownership of the mineral rights in the area have caused great friction over the years. The manors of Mold, Hope and Hawarden in Flintshire belonged to the Earl of Derby, but were lost when the Seventh Earl picked the wrong side in the Civil War. Only Hope was recovered. The shares of Mold were subdivided, the owners having the title of the 'Lords of Mold'. In Denbighshire, the mineral rights of the Lordships of Bromfield and Yale passed to the Grosvenor family in 1601 and the two rival factions, the Lords of Mold and the Grosvenors (later Dukes of Westminster), conducted an acrimonious dispute over who had the rights to win minerals in the mines at Cathole and on Pilkington's and Limekiln Rakes.

The Grosvenors had begun mining these sites in the 1720s, but after several decades of legal skirmishes they were 'evicted' by the Lords of Mold. The county boundary had always been obscure in law and litigation ensued in earnest in 1752. Many witnesses were called to certify where the boundary was, with some bizarre testimonies. The most notable were from those who had taken part as young children in 'beating the bounds'. Beating was meant quite literally, for when the young unfortunates were taken to each marker they were unceremoniously beaten so that the exact location would be indelibly printed on their mind.

In 1763 it was established by the Court of Exchequer in Westminster that a boulder called *Carreg Carn March Arthur* ('the stone of the hoof-print of Arthur's horse') was indeed the boundary and that the Lords of Mold had won the case. To commemorate the occasion and specify the line between the two mineral rights, a monument was erected in the same year on the spot above the stone, traditionally now the boundary between the counties of Flintshire and Denbighshire.

The monument (re-positioned because of road-widening) can be seen outside the Loggerheads Country Park by the side of the Mold to Ruthin Road (the present A494), and is another enigmatic reference to King Arthur, a name that occurs in the area's legend. With inspection the stone can be seen to have an indentation on its surface. This is, according to myth, the footprint of King Arthur's horse, caused when the animal jumped from the summit of Moel Famau, which towers above the site, and landed on the stone (Figure 66). The name 'Loggerheads' itself reflects such acrimonious struggles over the years. The inscription on the monument reads:

> The stone underneath this arch
> CARREG CARN MARCH ARTHUR
> was Adjuged to be the boundary of the
> Parish and Lordship of Mold in the County
> of Flint and of Llanverras in the County
> of Denbigh by the High Court of Exchequer
> at Westminster 10th November 1763.

FIGURE 66.
The *Carreg Carn March Arthur* boundary stone at Loggerheads.

The nature of the mines and water-courses in the Alun valley is complicated and need not concern us in detail here, being excellently described by Chris Williams (1979, 1997). Williams shows how Pen-y-fron, Llyn-y-pandy and Glan Alun mines illustrate the problem of dealing with excess water which plagued operations at the time.

Pen-y-fron Mine, at the west end of the Bryncelyn Vein, is located on the east bank of the Alun, just before it leaves the Clwydian Range at Rhydymwyn. By the late eighteenth century it had made the fortune of Richard Ingleby who with no more than pick-axe, windlass, bucket and wheel-barrow, produced up to 100 tons per week (Williams 1979, 65). By 1786 he was smelting at the site with a rolling-mill downstream and sending sheets to Flint and the sea for export. The problem of excess water began to assume more prominence as the enterprise got bigger. The installation of pumps, water-wheels and later a steam engine could not solve the problem and by the 1820s output had virtually ceased.

Upstream of Pen-y-fron, at Llyn-y-pandy, the great ironmaster John Wilkinson, of Brosely and Bersham fame, encountered the same difficulty. Wilkinson, who made cylinders for his friend James Watt's steam engines as well as cannon for the Peninsular War (Palmer 1899, 14–16), had by 1800 six engines at work at the site.

During the Napoleonic Wars demand for lead sank and many miners in the Clwydian Range were thrown out of work. As a result of an Act of Parliament of 1792, areas of waste were enclosed and much of Mold Mountain (land to the east of the Alun) was converted to agriculture. By the time of Wilkinson's death in 1808, Llyn-y-pandy seems to have been abandoned, but successive companies between 1876 and 1906 again produced appreciable quantities of ore.

Loggerheads Country Park contains the remains of the Loggerheads and Pen-y-garreg Mine (later called the Glan Alun Mine) on the west side of the Cathole Vein, and its waste tips, water-courses and wheel pits can still be seen. The mine was opened up, shafts sunk, levels driven and worked initially between 1769 and 1777 and a water-wheel installed on the east bank of the river to work water-pumps in the Pen-y-garreg shaft, located on top of the hill-side on the same bank. This was achieved by attaching flat-rods to run up a gully cut especially to take them. The over-grown wheel-pit (re-built in 1864 to take a 40 horse power turbine) is still visible and the wheel was probably supplied with water by means of a leat (cut water-course) several hundred metres long, also along the east bank. Without such equipment the mines would have quickly become flooded but it was expensive; the wheel cost £35 and the wooden pumps themselves cost £42 18s. 8d., with 15s. set aside for ale for the miners in celebration (Williams 1979, 64–65).

Despite all of this outlay, the mine made a loss and later the Glan Alun Mining Company took charge. By 1863 they had installed another wheel pit and wheel to pump water from the Glyn Alun adit, serviced by a leat, but by 1870 this had been superseded by another larger wheel. This huge wheel,

12 m in diameter by 1.8 m wide, was installed in a wheel pit on the west bank of the river opposite to the adit and was fed by a leat as a continuation of the one that serviced the corn mill at Loggerheads itself (Figure 67). Flat-rods appear to have been used across the river and into the adit, whilst a launder took water across the river again to a building below Pen-y-garreg shaft where the eighteenth-century waterwheel was situated. The mine closed in 1878.

The later fortunes of lead mining in the area, and some of the most

FIGURE 67.
This large pit at Loggerheads housed a 12 metre water-powered wheel to pump water from the Glyn Alun adit on the opposite bank of the River Alun.

important features of its history visible today, are intricately woven with John Taylor (1779–1863), a mining entrepreneur from Norfolk. Beginning his career at one of the largest mines in Devon, 'Wheal Friendship', he progressed to London in 1812, becoming mineral agent to the Earl Grosvenor and Duke of Devonshire. Between 1823 and 1845 virtually all of the mines in the area to the east of the Alun were consolidated into one enterprise, 'Mold Mines', as a result of Taylor's work and financial contacts, the 200 shares being entirely held by outsiders; a divergence from earlier days when local gentry were

FIGURE 68.
The 'Leete' watercourse
alongside the River
Alun, the masterpiece
of John Taylor, opened
in 1824.

prominent, such as Squire Yorke of Erddig, near Wrexham. A great deal of money was spent getting things off the ground and Williams (1979, 70) quotes a figure of £160,333 spent for a return of only £40,969 in the first four years of operation to 1825.

The water problem was the cause of these high costs and by 1829 seven steam engines and four waterwheels were in operation in the area, Taylor stating that at some 8,000 gallons of water a minute, this was the highest amount of water pumped in Britain. He was enthusiastic about the use of water-power and in 1824, his most visible legacy, 'The Leete' water channel, began to take water from just downstream at Loggerheads to the dressing floor at Pen-y-fron Mine (Figure 68). This quite considerable engineering feat was up to about 2 m wide and 1.5 m in depth and was constructed beside and then above the Alun itself. A series of additional leats supplied other wheels and uses.

John Taylor was a cultivated man from a non-conformist family. He rented Coed Du at Rhydymwyn, a large five-bayed house of 1813–1867 with an Italianate tower. There he entertained widely and in 1829 was host to the composer Felix Mendelssohn, who was inspired by the Alun to compose the piano fantasy *The Rivulet*. Another guest at Coed Du was Charles Kingsley who was a Canon of Chester Cathedral between 1870 and 1873. The author of *The Water Babies*, he took inspiration from the Leete and the river. Both visits are commemorated by a plaque in the village.

Associated with the veins of lead, the winning of other minerals in the Alun valley have resulted in spectacular relict features in the landscape; perhaps the most notable being the gorge cut into the steep east bank caused by the extraction of calcite (calcspar) and which now goes by the name of 'Devil's Gorge' (Figure 69).

It was not until the last century, however, that the problem of excess water was alleviated by the construction of two drainage tunnels, the 'Halkyn Deep Level' and the 'Milwr'. Both are great feats of engineering. The former had been started much earlier in 1818 by Earl Grosvenor for his Halkyn mines but was intermittently extended to reach the South Llyn-y-pandy mine in 1903. The later Milwr tunnel, begun in 1897, was again initially to drain the Halkyn mines, but the needs of the Great War resulted in greater lead output and extensions to the tunnel. Despite all of this, water still continued to be a problem and during the 1930s the Halkyn District United Mines company made abortive attempts to prevent water sinking through the natural swallow holes in the bed of the Alun at Loggerheads and so entering the mines further downstream. Extensions to the Milwr tunnel continued over the next 40 years, reaching the Cathole Vein and Loggerheads in 1958. By then the demand for lead was diminishing and the mining of lead finally finished in the Clwydian Range shortly afterwards.

The advent of lead mining spawned development in villages such as Maeshafn, to the east of Loggerheads. The mine there had been first worked in the eighteenth century, but was re-opened in 1823. Rows of miners cottages

FIGURE 69.
The former calcite mine at the 'Devil's Gorge'.

are grouped around what was once an engine house. On the east bank of the Alun to the north-west of the village, stood two large wheels. One, probably overshot, supplied power to a shaft to the east and the other, probably undershot, powered ore-dressing machinery (Hubbard 1986, 250 after Williams pers. comm.).

The engine house

There are excellent examples throughout the Clwydian Range of that most definitive feature of the lead-mining past in the landscape: the engine house

with its associated chimney. Examples are to the west of Eryrys at Nant, the Clive engine house at the Talargoch mine just below Graig Fawr between Dyserth and Meliden and the lead, silver and barytes mine at Pennant near Rhuallt (Figure 64).

Engine houses were built to house the steam-powered beam engines that operated the pumping machinery to extract water from the mines and to provide power. The nearby Flint and Denbigh coalfield accelerated the trend to steam from water power. The cylinder was inside the structure and the beam itself (some weighing 50 tons plus) protruded from an opening at the top side of the house. As steam entered the cylinder the piston pulled the beam downwards and when the steam was expelled rods attached to the beam outside the building worked pumps inside the shaft below. The reconstructed Meadow Shaft engine house at Minera near Wrexham of around 1905 shows this well. Another example in the Clwydian Range is at Pant Du on Nercwys Mountain, which has substantial remains which are now surrounded by tree growth. It was constructed of stone and brick and engine bases, flues and a wheel pit are still visible. The barytes mine at Pennant mine, north-east of Rhuallt, has evidence of foundations of the machinery and pumping mechanism, together with a leat, shafts, incline, cistern and trackways and the bases of a grinding mill, jigs and machinery mounts and bolts.

The Belgrave mine, which exploited the Belgrave Vein which runs from the River Alun to the Cefn-y-fedw sandstone, is located just north of Eryrys, to the west of Nercwys Mountain. Substantial evidence of its structure is recorded. It operated from the early nineteenth century till about 1857 for lead and silver with two engine house complexes. The eastern house pumped the main drawing shaft by means of flat rods and winding gear, with the boiler house as a platform on the southern side. A horse whim circle can be seen located to the east of the pumping house aligned to a capped shaft located to the east of it. A large complex of buildings is in evidence on the north side of the main mine track and is recorded on the Ordnance Survey map of 1874. Shafts and trials, ore-bin, leat, reservoir and foundations of cottages and office complex also remain (Figure 70).

The railways

The Mold and Denbigh Junction Railway, which traverses the northern edge of the Clwydian Range, opened in 1869 and was operated by the London and North Western Railway. It remained independent till the Railways Act of 1921 when it was incorporated as a subsidiary company in the London, Midland and Scottish Railway Company. Denbigh was then linked with Chester. Passenger traffic ceased in 1962 and the line lifted to Dolfechlas Crossing near Rhydymwyn under the Beeching proposals, but vestiges of the line and infrastructure still remain in the landscape, particularly in the form of buildings. The former station at Bodfari, now a private house but still with its railway character, is one such example. Regrettably the station at Nannerch, of similar

FIGURE 70.
The substantial remains of the Belgrave Mine, which exploited the Belgrave Vein for lead and silver till about 1857, are now overgrown.

design, was demolished for a road-widening scheme, and only part of an avenue of trees and shed remain (Figure 71). The line never achieved its true potential (Rear 2003, 27).

The Prestatyn and Dyserth Railway opened for stone and mineral traffic in 1869 (Thompson 1978; Rear 2003), skirting the Clwydian Range at its northern base. It served the quarries at Moel Hirraddug, Dyserth Castle and Graig Fawr which have had such deleterious effects on the landscape and archaeology of the Range. Basic passenger services opened in 1905, with seven halts, but closed as early as 1930, with freight and minerals remaining. Gradients were steep and curves sharp, necessitating speed restrictions as the lower slopes were climbed. The line finally closed to all traffic in 1974 and is now a public path (Figure 72).

FIGURE 71.
The former railway station site at Nannerch on the Mold and Denbigh Junction Railway.

FIGURE 72.
The line of the Prestatyn–Dyserth Railway, now a public footpath.

CHAPTER 12

Postscript:
Tea and Landscape Paintings

At the end of a grassy climb we reached the summit of Moel
Famau. What a view! The Clwydian Hills are the highest between
the Snowdon range and the Derbyshire Peak ... as we raced
down to Tafarn Gelyn at a good pace I thought that in the
autumn, when the heather is purple, this view from Moel Famau
must be one of the glories of Wales. (H. V. Morton 1932, 49)

Loggerheads has always been a special place in the hearts of, not only those
who live in the Clwydian Range, but also the many thousands from the conurbations of Merseyside, Manchester and Birmingham who have visited the site
and surrounding area since before the Second World War. As we have seen
the limestone scenery and River Alun have inspired many artists, writers and
musicians (Figure 74, page 163), but there is one who deserves a special mention. As well as the history of lead mining, Loggerheads is synonymous with
two things: Richard Wilson and tea.

Richard Wilson

Richard Wilson R.A. was born in 1713 (or 1714) at Penegoes in Montgomeryshire where his father, John, became rector in 1711, having previously been
Rector of Gwaenysgor in 1709. Probably educated at home, in 1729 he became
a pupil of the portrait painter Thomas Wright in London, paid for by his
cousin Sir George Wynne. From 1735 he was working on his own. He had
turned to landscape painting before he toured Italy (Venice, Rome,
Campagna), from 1750 to around 1757, where he became influenced by the
classic Italy of Gaspar Poussin and Claude Lorraine and the 'picturesque' landscapes of Vernet and Zuccarelli and Cuyp of the seventeenth-century Dutch
School. From then on he decided to devote himself to landscape painting. He
became a painter of the English school and was a Founder-Member of the
Royal Academy in 1768, being appointed its librarian in 1778. He can also
claim credit for starting the fashion for Welsh mountain landscapes. His paintings achieved a pure classicism, very atmospheric and full of light, a technique

learnt from the Dutch School as well as Claude. Both Constable and Turner were influenced by his style. The landscapes were largely ignored at the time, however, and trips to the pawnbroker with paintings still wet on the canvas were not unknown.

At the death of his brother a small estate came to him and he was invited to stay at Colomendy with the Jones family, his aunt and cousins, and there he remained for the last years of his life. It was during his time at Colomendy that he painted the famous 'We Three Loggerheads' signboard for the nearby Loggerheads Inn. Tradition has it that it was painted in lieu of money owed to the landlord (he had painted at least two other such signs), although Wilson himself said that it was done purely to amuse himself and others. Of two rather disgruntled men back to back, the third person in the picture 'at loggerheads' is of course the beholder. His poignant end is worthy of the great man – tradition has it that he had been out for a stroll along the Alun at Loggerheads surrounded by the scenery that he loved so much, when he collapsed. His dog ran back to the Hall, but when help reached him it was too late. He is buried at Mold and a plaque to his memory is in St Mary's Church.

Of tea and sunny days

In 1926 the Loggerheads Estate came up for sale and the Crosville Motor Company purchased land in the Alun valley for £1,600 to develop the site and transport visitors from Merseyside and the local area. The 'Crosville Tea House' at Loggerheads was born. No expense was spared. A wooden building was constructed with oak-block floor and open fireplace with copper canopy bearing the initials C.M.C., at a total cost approaching £7,000. The Tea Gardens were laid out in a semi-urban style with flower beds and lawns and in 1930 a bandstand was erected. Lobster sandwiches and mock turtle soup were served at 6*d.* each.

Initially the enterprise failed to make money, but with the advent of a new manageress, a Miss Jenkins, things looked up. Copeland Spode china replaced the former cheap crockery; flowers from the gardens grown by the head-gardener, Mr Corfield, were sold and the re-vamped building was re-christened the 'Loggerheads Road House'. It became famous and was the venue for weddings, local dances and other functions. Clock golf and croquet were played and Mr Dean from Park House next door built a children's boating lake which operated till 1962: 10 minutes for 1/6*d.* (Clwyd County Council 1987, 25–26).

The development at Loggerheads, whilst seeming quaint and nostalgic today, was entirely in-keeping with the spirit of the age and with the need of the urban dweller to experience the freedom of the countryside. The site gave hours of pleasure to the many thousands of visitors who came, whilst generating extra business for Crosville, as well as helping local employment. The bus service from Birkenhead, for example, doubled in frequency – both single and double-deckers arriving every hour from 7 a.m. till 10.20 at night. It was in fact a country park in all but name.

It is possible that a mill was sited at Loggerheads in early times and an Ingleby print dated 1796 features a mill with wheel. However, it is likely that the present Pentre Mill, now part of the Loggerheads Country Park and owned by Denbighshire County Council, dates from the early nineteenth century (Figure 75). Water comes via the mill race the 183 m from the Alun to a mill pond and thence to the over-shot wheel. Over the years the mill has seen a variety of uses; for flour as well as timber. A saw pit was installed in 1871 when a William Williams, carpenter, took over the site. In 1900 the mill was

FIGURE 73.
Roman enactments are a popular summer feature at the Loggerheads Country Park.

acquired by David Williams and he and his family continued working at the mill until the 1940s. The mill derived its power from the water wheel for grinding, sawing and producing electricity till 1942 (Davies 1986, 2).

In 1974 the new Clwyd County Council, formed as a result of the amalgamation of Denbighshire and Flintshire County Councils, bought the site for a country park with the assistance of the Countryside Commission. The Tea Gardens continued to prove popular with visitors but, in 1984, a fire gutted the wooden road house. Out of the ashes rose the new Loggerheads

FIGURE 74.
The Loggerheads
Rocks. The epitome of
the Loggerheads
Country Park.

IAN BROWN

Countryside Centre which we see today and which, 77 years after Crosville first bought the site, is still as popular as ever, functioning as a 'gateway' to the cultural and natural heritage of the Clwydian Range (Figure 73).

AONBs and the Clwydian Range

The concept of Areas of Outstanding Natural Beauty came out of the National Parks and Access to the Countryside Act, 1949. This is a *national* designation to conserve the most important landscape of the nation for the benefit of this

FIGURE 75.
The Loggerheads Mill in 1973 before restoration by Clwyd County Council.

IAN BROWN

and future generations. The conservation and enhancement of this natural beauty, which includes the protection of flora, fauna and geological as well as landscape features, is the primary aim, but, as the landscape has been shaped by past human influence, the conservation of archaeological and historic sites, landscapes and architectural and vernacular features, is no less important. AONBs are therefore every bit as significant as National Parks in terms of quality of the landscape.

The Clwydian Range is one of five AONBs in Wales, the others being the Llŷn, Anglesey, Gower and the Welsh section of the Wye Valley, but these form part of a much wider family of 41 such designated areas throughout England and Wales. All of these are subject to pressures of recreation, intensive farming, transport, settlement and industry that have led to substantial deterioration in landscape quality over the years since the Second World War.

Such areas do not look after themselves and local authorities are now statutorily charged with producing management plans setting out how things should be cared for in the future. The Clwydian Range has been at the forefront of AONB awareness nationally and since its inception has set up mechanisms to involve the community in schemes and programmes. What is required is involvement by all in a shared appreciation of a landscape that has been shaped by the hands of countless people since the Stone Age. It is hoped that this book will assist in this process. The clues to our heritage are out there – and you can go and find them for yourself.

Bibliography

Aldhouse-Green, S. H. R. (2000) 'The Palaeolithic Period', in Lynch, F. M., Aldhouse-Green, S. H. R. and Davies, J. L. *Prehistoric Wales*. Sutton Publishing. Stroud. 1–22.

Aldhouse-Green, S. H. R., Pettitt, P. and Stringer, C. B. (1996) 'Holocene hominids at Pontnewydd and Cae Gronw'. *Antiquity*, 70, 444–47.

Arnold, C. J. and Davies, J. L. (2000) *Roman and early medieval Wales*. Sutton Publishing. Stroud.

Ashton, N. (2003) 'Hunting for the first humans in Britain'. *British Archaeology*, 70, 8–13.

Barker, P. and Higham, R. (1982) *Hen Domen, Montgomery*. R. A. I. London.

Barker, P. and Higham, R. (1988) *A timber castle on the English-Welsh border, Hen Domen Archaeological Project*. Hen Domen Archaeological Project.

Barnatt, J. (1996) 'Moving beyond the monuments: paths and people in the Neolithic landscapes of the Peak District', in Frodsham, P. (ed.) *Neolithic studies in No-Man's-Land; Papers on the Neolithic of northern England from the Trent to the Tweed*. Northern Archaeology, 13/14, 43–60.

Barnatt, J. (1998) 'Monuments in the landscape: thoughts from the Peak', in Gibson, A. and Simpson, D. (eds) *Prehistoric ritual and religion*. Sutton Publishing. Stroud. 92–105.

Beer, A. W. (1919–20) 'The church of St Mary Magdalene, Gwaenysgor'. *Journal of the Flintshire Historical Society*, 7, 1–21.

Benson, D. G., Evans, J. G., Williams, G. H., Darvill, T. and David, A. (1990) 'Excavations at Stackpole Warren, Dyfed'. *Proceedings of the Prehistoric Society*, 56, 179–245.

Berry, A. Q. B. (1994) 'The parks and forests of the Lordship of Dyffryn Clwyd'. *Denbighshire Historical Society Transactions*, 43, 7–25.

Bevan-Evans, M. and Hayes, P. (1952–3) 'Excavation of a cairn on Cefn-Goleu near Moel Famau'. *Flintshire Historical Society Publications*, 13, 91–97.

Bevan-Evans, M. and Hayes, P. (1954–5) 'Excavation of a cairn on Cefn-Goleu, near Moel Famau – 2nd Report'. *Flintshire Historical Society Publications*, 15, 112–40.

Black, A. and Black. C. (1874) *Black's picturesque guide through Wales*. Adam and Charles Black. Edinburgh.

Blockley, K. (1985) 'Excavations on the Roman civil settlement at Prestatyn'. *Archaeology in Clwyd*, 7, 12–15.

Blockley, K. (1986) 'Further excavations on the Roman civil settlement at Prestatyn 1985'. *Archaeology in Clwyd*, 8, 7.

Blockley, K. (1989) *Prestatyn 1984–5. An Iron Age farmstead and Romano-British industrial settlement in North Wales*. Oxford.

Blockley, K. (1991) 'The Romano-British period', in Manley, J., Grenter, S. and Gale, F. (eds) *The archaeology of Clwyd*. Clwyd County Council. Mold. 117–128.

Blore, J. D. (2002) *The enigmatic lynx*. Wallasey.

Boon, G. C. (1968) 'The Penard Roman Imperial hoard: An interim report and a list of Roman hoards in Wales'. *Bulletin Board of Celtic Studies*, XXII, 291–310.

Borrow, G. (1862) *Wild Wales*. Bridge Books edition 2002. Wrexham.

Branigan, K. and Dearne, M. J. (1992). *Romano-British cavemen. Cave use in Roman Britain*. Oxbow Monograph 19. Oxford.

Brassil, K. S. (1987) 'Tandderwen, Denbigh: a Dark Age cemetery in the middle of Dyffryn Clwyd'. *Archaeology in Clwyd*, 9, 6–8.

Bibliography

Brassil, K. S. (1991) 'Mesolithic', in Manley, J., Grenter, S. and Gale, F. (eds) *The archaeology of Clwyd*. Clwyd County Council. Mold. 47–54.

Brassil, K. S. and Guilbert, G. C. (1982) 'Caves in Clwyd'. *Archaeology in Clwyd*, 4, 4–5.

Brassil, K. S., Guilbert, G. C., Livens, R. G., Stead, W. H. and the late Bevan-Evans, M. (1982) 'Rescue excavations at Moel Hiraddug between 1960 and 1980'. *Journal of the Flintshire Historical Society*, 30, 13–88.

Briffa, K. and Atkinson, T. (1997) 'Re-constructing Late-Glacial and Holocene climates', in Hulme, M. and Barrow, E. (eds) *Climates of the British Isles present, past and future*. Routledge. London. 84–111.

Britnell, J. (1990) 'Settlement and trade in north-east Wales', in Burnham, B. and Davies, J. L. (eds) (1990) *Conquest, co-existence and change. Recent work in Roman Wales*. Trivium, 25, Lampeter.

Brown, E. H. (1960) *The relief and drainage of Wales*. University of Wales Press. Cardiff.

Brown, I. W., Ratcliffe, J. B. and Hawkes, D. E. (1979) *Moel Famau Country Park Management Plan. Environmental resource analysis*. Clwyd County Council. Mold.

Brown, I. W., Ratcliffe, J. B. and Hawkes, D. E. (1980) 'The development of a spatial resource inventory system for countryside planning purposes in the Clwydian Hills of North Wales'. *Landscape Research*, 5, 20–23.

Brown, I. W. and Wathern, P. (1985) 'Bracken control and land management in the Moel Famau Country Park, Clwyd, North Wales', in Smith, R. T. and Taylor, J. A. (eds) *Bracken. Ecology, land use and control technology*. Parthenon Publishing. Carnforth. 369–377.

Burgess, C. B., Coombs, D. G. and Davies, D. G. (1972) 'The Broadward Complex and barbed spearheads', in Lynch, F. M. and Burgess, C. B. (eds) *Prehistoric man in Wales and the West: Essays in honour of Lily F. Chitty*. Adams and Dart. Bath.

Burl, A. (1995) *A guide to the stone circles of Britain, Ireland and Brittany*. Yale University Press.

Burnham, B. and Davies, J. L. (eds) (1990) *Conquest, co-existence and change. Recent work in Roman Wales*. Trivium, 25, Lampeter.

Burnham, H. (1995) *A guide to ancient and historic Wales. Clwyd and Powys*. HMSO. London.

CADW/ICOMOS UK (1995) *Clwyd register of landscapes, parks and gardens of special historic interest in Wales, Pt. 1: Parks and gardens*. CADW. Cardiff.

Camden (1600) *Britannia*. Edition of 1600 (quoted in Davies, Canon Ellis 1949, 185).

Cathcart King, D. (1991) 'The stone castles', in Manley, J., Grenter, S. and Gale, F. (eds) *The archaeology of Clwyd*. Clwyd County Council. Mold. 173–185.

Chamberlain, A. T. and Williams, J. P. (2002) *A gazetteer of Welsh caves, fissures and rock shelters containing human remains*. Capra 2 available at http://www.shef.ac.uk/~capra/2/wales. html

Chambers, F. M. and Lageard, J. G. A. (1993) 'Vegetational history and environmental setting of Crawcwellt, Gwynedd'. *Archaeology in Wales*, 33, 23–5.

Chambers, F. M. and Price, S. M. (1988) 'The environmental setting of Erw-wen and Moel y Gerddi: prehistoric enclosures in upland Ardudwy, North Wales'. *Proceedings of the Prehistoric Society*, 54, 93–100.

Clark, G. (1940) *Prehistoric England*. Batsford. London.

Clark, J. D. G. (1938) 'Microlithic industries from tufa deposits at Prestatyn, Flintshire and Blashenwell, Dorset'. *Proceedings of the Prehistoric Society*, IV, 330–34.

Clwyd County Council (undated) *Pentre Mill, Loggerheads*. Clwyd County Council. Mold.

Clwyd County Council (undated) *Prehistoric Rhyl*. Clwyd County Council. Mold.

Clwyd County Council (undated) *Hill farming in Clwyd*. Clwyd County Council. Mold.

Clwyd County Council (1987) *Loggerheads in old postcards*. Clwyd County Council. Mold.

Clwyd County Council (1995) *Clwydian upland survey Phase 2 1994/5*. Clwyd County Council, Mold.

Clwyd Powys Archaeological Trust (2003) *Projects – historic landscapes – The Vale of Clwyd*. Available at http://www.cpat.org.uk/projects/longer/histland/clwyd/clwyd.htm

Collis, J. (1996) 'The origin and spread of the Celts'. *Studia Celtica*, XXX, 17–34.

Cunliffe, B. W. (1991) *Iron Age communities in Britain*. 3rd. Edition. Routledge. London.

Cunliffe, B. W. (1993) *Fertility, propitiation and the gods in the British Iron Age*. Vijftiende Kroon-Voordracht. Universiteit van Amsterdam.

Cunliffe, B. W. (1995) *Iron Age Britain*. Batsford/English Heritage. London.

Cunliffe, B. W. (1997) *The ancient celts*. Oxford University Press. Oxford.

Cunliffe, B. W. (2001) *Facing the ocean*. Oxford University Press. Oxford.

Dark, P. (2000) *The environment of Britain in the first millennium AD*. Duckworth. London.

Darvill, T. (1987) *Prehistoric Britain*. Routledge. London.

Davies, D. G. (1967) 'The Guilsfield hoard: a reconsideration'. *Antiquaries Journal*, 47, 95–108.

Davies, Canon Ellis (1929) *Prehistoric and Roman remains of Denbighshire*. William Lewis. Cardiff.

Davies, Canon Ellis (1949) *Prehistoric and Roman remains of Flintshire*. William Lewis. Cardiff.

Davies, J. I. (1986) *The last miller*. Clwyd County Council. Mold.

Davies, M. (1975) 'Ogof Colomendy'. Archaeology in Wales, 15, 23–24.

Davies, M. (1976) 'Ogof Colomendy'. Archaeology in Wales, 16, 20.

Davies, M. (1977) 'Ogof Colomendy'. Archaeology in Wales, 17, 20.

Davies, M. (1989) 'Cave archaeology in North Wales', in Ford, T. D. (ed.) *Limestones and caves of Wales*. Cambridge University Press. 92–101.

Davies, J. L. and Lynch, F. M. (2000) 'The Late Bronze Age and Iron Age', in Lynch, F. M., Aldhouse-Green, S. H. R. and Davies, J. L. *Prehistoric Wales*. Sutton Publishing. Stroud. Stroud. 139–219.

Dawkins, W. B. (1874) *Cave hunting*. Macmillan. London.

Dawkins, W. B. (1901) 'On the cairn and sepulchral cave at Gop, near Prestatyn'. *Archaeologia Cambrensis*, 6th. series 11, 161–81.

Denbighshire County Council (1997) *Clwydian Range upland survey 1996–7. An archaeological survey*. Denbighshire County Council, Ruthin.

Denbighshire County Council (1998) *Clwydian Range upland survey 1997–8. An archaeological survey*. Denbighshire County Council, Ruthin.

Denbighshire County Council (2000) *Clwydian Range Area of Outstanding Natural Beauty Management Strategy*. Denbighshire County Council. Ruthin.

Dyer, J. (1990) *Ancient Britain*. Batsford, London (re-printed Routledge, London 1997).

Edwards, N. (1991) 'The dark ages', in Manley, J., Grenter, S. and Gale, F. (eds) *The archaeology of Clwyd*. Clwyd County Council. Mold. 129–144.

Eogan, G. (1986) *Knowth and the passage tombs of Ireland*. Thames and Hudson. London.

Evans, E. D. (2001) 'The Crown lordships of Denbighshire'. *Denbighshire Historical Society Transactions*, 9, 24–36.

Evans, Sir J. (1872) *The ancient stone implements, weapons and ornaments of Great Britain*. London.

Field, D. (2003) 'Silbury Hill'. *British Archaeology*, 70, 14–17.

Fisher, J. (ed.) (1917) *Tours in Wales (1804–1813) by Richard Fenton*. Cambrian Archaeological Association/Bedford Press. London.

Fleming, L. and Gore, A. (1988) *The English garden*. Spring Books. London.

Forde-Johnston, J. (1964a) 'A hoard of flat axes from Moel Arthur'. *Journal of the Flintshire Historical Society*, 21, 99–100.

Forde-Johnston, J. (1964b) 'Fieldwork on the hillforts of North Wales'. *Journal of the Flintshire Historical Society*, 21, 1–20.

Forde-Johnston, J. (1976) *Prehistoric Britain and Ireland*. Dent. London.

Gamble, C. (1994) 'The peopling of Europe 700,000–40,000 years before the present', in Cunliffe, B. W. (ed.) *The Oxford illustrated pre-history of Europe*. Oxford University Press. Oxford. 5–41.

Gardner, W. (1926) 'The native hillforts of North Wales and their defences'. *Archaeologia Cambrensis*, 7th series Vol. 6, 221–282.

Gilks, J. (1989) 'Cave burials in Northern England'. *British Archaeology*, 11, 11–15.

Glenn, T. A. (1914) 'Exploration of a Neolithic station near Gwaenysgor, Flints'. *Archaeologia Cambrensis*, 14, 247–70.

Bibliography

Glenn, T. A. (1915) 'Prehistoric and historic remains at Dyserth Castle'. *Archaeologia Cambrensis*, 6, 47–86.

Glenn, T. A. (1935) 'Distribution of the Graig Lwyd axe and its associated cultures'. *Archaeologia Cambrensis*, 90, 189–214.

Green, H. S. (1982) 'A Late Bronze Age hoard from Llanarmon-yn-Iâl'. *Archaeology in Clwyd*, 1982.

Green, H. S. (1984) 'The Late Bronze Age hoard from Llanarmon yn Iâl, Clwyd'. *Antiquaries Journal*, 63, 384–87.

Green, M. (1986) *The gods of the Celts*. Alan Sutton. Stroud.

Green, M. (1992) *Animals in Celtic life and myth*. Routledge. London.

Green, M. and Howell, R. (2000) *A pocket guide to Celtic Wales*. University of Wales Press/ Western Mail. Cardiff.

Green, S. (1991) 'The Palaeolithic and its Quaternary context', in Manley, J., Grenter, S. and Gale, F. (eds) *The archaeology of Clwyd*. Clwyd County Council. Mold. 26–46.

Grenter, S. (1989) 'Gwernymynydd axe hoard'. *Archaeology in Wales*, 29, 46.

Grenter, S. and Williams A. Lloyd (1991) 'Clwyd in the Industrial Revolution', in Manley, J., Grenter, S. and Gale, F. (eds) *The archaeology of Clwyd*. Clwyd County Council. Mold. 219–230.

Griffiths, R. (2001) 'Wales from conquest to union 1282–1536', in Morgan, P. (ed.) *The Tempus history of Wales 25,000 BC–AD 2000*. Tempus/National Library of Wales. Stroud. 107–140.

Guilbert, G. (1976) 'Moel y Gaer (Rhosesmor) 1972–1973: an area excavation in the interior', in Harding, D. W. (ed.) *Hillforts: later prehistoric earthworks in Britain and Ireland*. Academic Press. London. 303–17.

Guilbert, G. (1982a) 'Orchid Cave'. *Archaeology in Wales*, 22, 15.

Guilbert, G. (1982b) 'Iron-Age artefacts from Moel Hiraddug'. *Archaeology in Clwyd*, 1982, 12–14.

Hemp, W. J. (1928) 'A La Tène shield from Moel Hiraddug, Flintshire'. *Archaeologia Cambrensis*, 83, 252–84.

Hesketh, G. E. (1954–55) 'An account of the excavations in the cave in Big Covert, Maeshafn, Llanferres'. *Flintshire Historical Society Publications*, 15, 141–48.

Higham, R. and Barker, P. (2000) *Hen Domen Montgomery: A Timber Castle on the English-Welsh Border*. University of Exeter Press. Exeter.

Houlder, C. H. (1961) 'The excavation of a Neolithic stone implement factory on Mynydd Rhiw in Caernarvonshire'. *Proceedings of the Prehistoric Society*, 27, 108–43.

Howell, D. W. (1979) 'The historical development of common land in Wales', in Bridges, E. M. (ed.) *Problems of common land: the example of West Glamorgan*. University College of Swansea. Swansea.

Howell, R. (2001) 'Roman Wales', in Morgan, P. (ed.) *The Tempus history of Wales 25,000 BC–AD 2000*. Tempus/National Library of Wales. Stroud. 39–46.

Hubbard, E. (1986) *The buildings of Wales. Clwyd (Denbighshire and Flintshire)*. Penguin Books. London.

Hutton, R. (1991) *The pagan religions of the Ancient British Isles their nature and legacy*. Blackwell. Oxford.

Irving, W. (1783–1859) *Sketch book*. Quoted by Robert, D. (ed.) (1992) *Visitor's delight. An anthology of visitors' impressions of North Wales*. Gwasg Carreg Gwalch. Llanrwst.

Ivinson, S. (2001) *Anglo-Welsh wars 1050–1300*. Bridge Books. Wrexham.

Jacobi, R. M. (1973) 'Aspects of the Mesolithic Age in Great Britain', in Kozlowski, S. *The Mesolithic in Europe*. 237–65.

James, S. (1999) *The Atlantic Celts. Ancient people or modern invention?* British Museum Press. London.

Jenkins, D., Lacelles, B. and Williams, J. (1995) 'Hiraethog's changing vegetation. *Clwyd Archaeology News*.

Jenkins, D. A. (1991) 'The environment: past and present', in Manley, J., Grenter, S. and Gale, F. (1991) *The archaeology of Clwyd*. Clwyd County Council. Mold. 13–25.

Jenkins, G. H. (2001) 'From reformation to Methodism 1536–c. 1750', in Morgan, P. (ed.) *The Tempus history of Wales 25,000 BC–AD 2000*. Tempus/National Library of Wales. Stroud. 141–174.

Jenner, L. (undated) *Explore Cwm, Waen and Tremeirchion*. Denbighshire County Council, Ruthin.

Jones, G. (1991) 'Medieval settlement', in Manley, J., Grenter, S. and Gale, F. (eds) (1991) *The archaeology of Clwyd*. Clwyd County Council. Mold. 186–202.

Jones. M. E. (1996) *The end of Roman Britain*. Cornell University Press.

Jope, E. M. (2000) *Early Celtic art in the British Isles*. Oxford University Press. Oxford.

Kelly, R. S. (1988) 'Two late prehistoric circular enclosures near Harlech, Gwynedd'. *Proceedings of the Prehistoric Society*, 54, 101–51.

Kendrick, T. D. (1928) *The Druids*. London.

Kingdon, J. (1993) *Self-made man and his undoing*. Simon and Schuster. London.

Landlow, G. P (2003) 'Ruskin on the picturesque', in *The aesthetic and critical theories of John Ruskin*. Available at http://65.107.211.206/authors/ruskin/atheories/3.2.html

Lewis, S. (1842) *Topographical Dictionary*.

Longworth, I. (1958) 'Notes on excavations in the British Isles, 1958'. *Proceedings of the Prehistoric Society*, 25, 280–81.

Lynch, F. M. (1969) 'The megalithic tombs of North Wales' and 'The contents of excavated tombs in North Wales', in Powell, T. G. E. (ed.) *Megalithic enquiries in the west of Britain*. 107–74.

Lynch, F. M. (1986) 'Archaeology and physical evidence for man in Wales', in Harper, P. S. and Sunderland, E. (eds) *Genetic and population studies in Wales*. University of Wales Press, Cardiff. 15–30.

Lynch, F. M. (1991) 'The Bronze Age', in Manley, J., Grenter, S. and Gale, F. *The archaeology of Clwyd*. Clwyd County Council. Mold. 65–81.

Lynch, F. M. (2000) 'The earlier Neolithic', in Lynch, F., Aldhouse-Green, S. and Davies, J. L. *Prehistoric Wales*. Sutton Publishing. Stroud. Stroud. 42–78.

Manley, J. (1989) 'Rhyl and coastal evolution'. *Journal of the Flintshire Historical Society*, 32, 181–89.

Manley, J., Grenter, S. and Gale, F. (1991) *The archaeology of Clwyd*. Clwyd County Council. Mold.

Manley, J. and Healey, E. (1982) 'Excavations at Hendre, Rhuddlan'. *Archaeologia Cambrensis*, CXXXI, 18–48.

Megaw, R. and Megaw, V. (1989) *Celtic art. From its beginnings to the Book of Kells*. Thames and Hudson.

Mighall, T. M. and Chambers, F. M. (1995) 'Holocene vegetational history and human impact at Bryn y Castell, Snowdonia, North Wales'. *New Phytologist*, 130, 299–321.

Miles, H. (1971–72) 'Excavations at Rhuddlan 1969–71: Interim Report'. *Journal of the Flintshire Historical Society*, 25, 1–8.

Moore-Colyer, R. (2002) *Welsh cattle drovers*. Landmark Publishing. Ashbourne.

Morton, H. V. (1932) *In search of Wales*. Methuen. London.

Musson, C. R., Britnell, W. J., Northover, J. P. and Salter, C. J. (1992) 'Excavations and metal working at Llwyn Bryn Dinas hillfort, Llangedwyn, Clwyd'. *Proceedings of the Prehistoric Society*, 58, 265–84.

Naphy, W. and Spicer, A. (2000) *The Black Death and the history of plagues 1345–1730*. Tempus. Stroud.

Needham, S. P., Lees, M. N., Hook, D. R. and Hughes, M. J. (1989) 'Developments in the Early Bronze Age metallurgy of Southern Britain'. *World Archaeology*, 20, 383–402.

Northover, J. P. (1995) 'Bronze Age gold in Britain', in Morteani, G. and Northover, J. P. (eds) *Prehistoric gold in Europe*. NATO ASI Series. Dortrecht. 515–31.

Ó hÓgáin, D. (2002) *The Celts: a history*. The Boydell Press. Woodbridge.

O'Neil, B. H. St J. (1942) 'Excavations at Ffridd Faldwyn Camp, Montgomery, 1937–39'. *Archaeologia Cambrensis*, 97, 1–57.

Bibliography

Owen, E. (late sixteenth century) *Cymmrodorion Record Series*, No. 5, p. 152. British Museum.

Owen, E. (1886) *Old stone crosses of the vale of Clwyd.* Clwyd County Council reprint 1995. Mold.

Owen, T. M. (1991) *The customs and traditions of Wales.* University of Wales Press/Western Mail. Cardiff.

Palmer, A. N. (1899) *John Wilkinson and the Old Bersham Ironworks.* Bridge Books edition 1988. Wrexham.

Parker, A. G. and Chambers, F. M. (1997) 'Late-Quaternary palaeoecology of the Severn, Wye and Upper Thames', in Lewis, S. G. and Maddy, D. (eds) *The Quaternary of the south Midlands and the Welsh Marches: Field Guide.* Quaternary Research Association.

Pennant, T. (1781) *Tours in Wales Vol. II.* Rhys, J. (ed. 1883). H. Humphreys. Caernarvon.

Pollard, A. E. (1912) *The history of England. A study in political evolution.* Williams and Norgate. London.

Powell, T. G. E. (1954) 'Excavations at Gwaenysgor (Flints.) 1951'. *Archaeologia Cambrensis*, 103, 109–11.

Powell, T. G. E. and Daniel, G. E. (1956) *Barcloddiad y Gawres.* Liverpool University Press. Liverpool.

Pratt, D. (1976) 'Minera: Township of the mines'. *Denbighshire Historical Society Transactions*, 25, 114–154.

Pratt, D. (1990) 'The lordship of Chirk'. *Denbighshire Historical Society Transactions*, 39, 5–41.

Pryce, A. H. (2001) 'Frontier Wales', in Morgan, P. (ed.) (2001) *The Tempus history of Wales 25,000 BC–AD 2000.* Tempus/National Library of Wales. Stroud. 77–106.

Quinell, H. and Blockley, M. with Berridge, P. (1994) *Excavations at Rhuddlan, Clwyd. 1969–73. Mesolithic to Medieval.* Council for British Archaeology, Research Report 95. London.

Read, H. and Stangos, N. (1993) *The Thames and Hudson dictionary of art and artists.* Thames & Hudson, London.

Rear, B. (2003) *From Chester to Holyhead. The branch lines.* Oxford Publishing Company. Hersham.

Rees, A. and Rees, B. (1961) *Celtic heritage. Ancient tradition in Ireland and Wales.* Thames and Hudson. London.

Renn, D. F. (1973) *Norman castles in Britain.* John Baker/Humanities Press. London.

Rivet, R. L. F. (1958) *Town and country in Roman Britain.* Hutchinson University Library. London.

Roberts, D. (1992) *An anthology of visitor's impressions of north Wales.* Gwasg Carreg Gwalch. Llanrwst.

Rolleston, T. W. (1911) *Celtic myths and legends.* Senate impression 1994. London.

Ross, A. (1998) *Pagan Celts.* John Jones re-print of Batsford, London 1970. Ruthin.

Rowley, T. (2001) *The Welsh border.* Tempus. Stroud.

Ruskin, J. (1880) *Frondes Agrestes.* George Allen. Orpington.

Savory, H. N. (1951) 'Excavations and discoveries. Burial cave at Llanferres (Denb.)'. *Bulletin Board of Celtic Studies*, XIV, 174–75.

Sheridan, A. and Davis, M. (2001) 'The Welsh 'Jet Set' in prehistory: a case of keeping up with the Joneses?', in Gibson, A. and Simpson, D. (eds) *Prehistoric ritual and religion.* Sutton Publishing. Stroud. 148–162.

Simmons, I. G. (1996) *The environmental impact of Later Mesolithic cultures: the creation of moorland landscape in England and Wales.* Edinburgh University Press. Edinburgh.

Simpson, F. (1912) *Cilcain and its parish church.* Address to the Flintshire Historical Society May 2nd. 1912. 58pp.

Smyth, J. (2000) 'Mottes and baileys', in Leonard, J., Preshous, D., Roberts, M., Smyth, J. and Train, C. (eds) *The gale of life. Two thousand years in south-west Shropshire.* South-West Shropshire Historical and Archaeological Society/Logaston Press. Logaston. 87–97.

Squire, C. (undated) *Celtic myth and legend.* Gresham Publishing Company. London.

Stapleton, P. (1909) 'Exploration of Moel-y-Gaer, Bodfari'. *Archaeologia Cambrensis*, 6th. Series, IX, 232–238.

Steane, J. (1985) *The archaeology of medieval England and Wales*. Croom Helm. London.

Stenton, F. (1943) *Anglo-Saxon England*. Oxford University Press. Oxford.

Sylvester, D. (1954–55) 'Settlement patterns in rural Flintshire'. *Flintshire Historical Society Publications*, 15, 6–42.

Taylor, A. (2001) *Burial practice in early England*. Tempus. Stroud.

Taylor, T. (1996) *The prehistory of sex*. Fourth Estate. London.

Thomas, Rev. A. (1971–72) 'G. M. Hopkins and St Beuno's College'. *Journal of the Flintshire Historical Society*, 25, 98–102.

Thomas, C. (2003) *Christian Celts*. Tempus. Stroud.

Thompson, T. (1976) *The Prestatyn and Dyserth Railway*. North Clwyd Railway Association.

Tooley, M. J. (1985) 'Sea-level changes and coastal morphology in North-west England', in Johnson, R. H. (ed.) *The geomorphology of North-West England*. Manchester. 94–121.

Toulson, S. and Forbes, C. (1992) *The drover's roads of Wales II. Pembrokeshire and the south*. Whittet Books. London.

Trevelyan, M. (undated) *The land of Arthur*. John Hogg. London.

Trump, D. (1957) 'Notes on excavations in the British Isles, 1957'. *Proceedings of the Prehistoric Society*, 24, 219.

Varley, W. J. (1935) 'Maiden Castle, Bickerton. Preliminary excavations, 1935'. *Annals of Archaeology and Anthropology*, Liverpool, 22, 1–2.

Varley, W. J. (1936) 'Further excavations at Maiden Castle, Bickerton, 1935'. *Annals of Archaeology and Anthropology*, Liverpool, 23, 3–4.

Watkins, R. (1990) 'The postglacial vegetational history of lowland Gwynedd – Llyn Cororion', in Addison, K., Edge, M. J. and Watkins, R. (eds) *North Wales Field Guide*. Quaternary Research Association. Coventry. 131–36.

Webster, G. (1975) *The Cornovii*. Duckworth. London.

Wells, A. K. and Kirkaldy, J. F. (1966) *Outline of historical geology*. Thomas Murby. London.

Williams, C. J. (1979) 'The lead mines of the Alyn valley'. *Journal of the Flintshire Historical Society*, 29, 51–87.

Williams, C. J. (1997) *The metal mines of North Wales*. Bridge Books. Wrexham.

Wynne Ffoulkes, Rev. W. (1850) 'Castra Clwydiana No. I. Moel Fenlli'. *Archaeologia Cambrensis*, New Series, I, 81–89.

Wynne Ffoulkes, Rev. W. (1850) 'Castra Clwydiana No. II. Moel Gaer, Part of Moel Fama'. *Archaeologia Cambrensis*, New Series, I, 174–87.

Index

....

Eryrys Mountain 25
Eurgain 112
European Lynx 25, 39
Evans, Sir John 71
Ewart Park phase 54
excarnation 40–1, 53, 93

feasting 62–3, 65–6
Fenton, Richard 117, 140
festivals 115–16
Ffair y bol 116
Ffridd Faldwyn 72
Ffrith vegetation 12, 130, 132
Ffrith, Prestatyn 29
Ffrith, Wrexham 86
Ffynnon Beuno Cave **18**, 19, 22, **23**, 24–5
Ffynnon Beuno (well) **127**, 128
field patterns (ancient) 120
Flanders (mercenaries) 101
Flavian period 86
Flemish migrants 100
Flint 86
Flint Castle 105
Flint and Denbigh Coalfield 12, 157
Flintshire pigs 86
Flintshire Plateau 6, 10, 78
Fox, Sir Cyril 55
free township 120

Gaer Fawr hoard 53
Gastineau, Henry 137
gavelkind (partible inheritance) 61, 99, 120,
    123, 125, 132
George III 141
Gilpin, Rev. William 135–6
Glan Alun adit 151–2
Glan Alun mines 151
Glan Alun Mining Company 151
Glenn, T. A. 41–2
Gloucester (*Glevum*) 94, 120
Glyndyfrdwy 105
gold mining 147
Golden Grove, Llanasa 125–6, **126**, 140
Gop Cairn 37–8, 40–1, **42**, 109, 113
Gop Cave(s) **34**, 35, 38
Gop Farm Cave (Gwenysgor Cave) 39
Gop Hill (The Gop) 13, 40, 45
Gordian III 87
Gosper canwyllau (Candle Vespers) 112
Gower AONB 165
Graigfechan 12
Graig, The 24
Graig Fawr 13, 4, 158

Graig Lwyd axe 35, 38, **39**, 40–2
Grand Tour 136
Grange (monastic) 107, 128
Greasby, Merseyside 31
Great Orme, Llandudno 89
Gresham, Thomas 139
Gritstone Hills 15, 17
Grosvenor family 149
Grosvenor, Earl of 153, 155
grottoes 140
Gruffudd ap Cynan 100
Gruffydd ap Ifan ap Llewelyn Vychan 117
Gruffudd ap Llywelyn 99
Gwaenysgor 41, 110, 117, 120, 160
Gwalchmai ap Meilyr 66
Gwelyau 119
Gwernymynyd 56
Gwestfa 120
Gwylmabsant 115
Gwynedd (native principality) 3, 99–101,
    103–4
Gwynedd Is-conwy 100

Hadrianic period 86
hafod 130
Halkyn Deep Level 155
Halkyn District United Mines 155
Halkyn Mountain 86
Hallstatt culture 53, 60
Hansom and Co. 141
Harlech Castle 105
Harrison, Thomas 141–2
Hawarden, manor of 149
Hearse house, Cilcain 110
Hendre, Rhuddlan 29–30
Hendr'r Ywydd Uchaf, Llangynhafal 125
Henry I 100
Henry II 100–1
Henry III 103
Henry IV 105–6
Henry V ('Prince Hal') 105–6, 135
Henry VI 106
Henry VII (Henry Tudor) 106, 123
Henry VIII 123, 127
Henry Hotspur 105
Henry de Lacy, Earl of Lincoln 105
Hen Domen 101–2
Herdwick flocks, Lake District 130
Hereford 99
hero's portion 62
Hill of the Arrows 37
Hillslopes 13
Hoare, Sir Richard Colt 137